Extending Symfony2 Web Application Framework

Optimize, audit, and customize web applications with Symfony

Sébastien Armand

BIRMINGHAM - MUMBAI

Extending Symfony2 Web Application Framework

First published: March 2014

Production Reference: 1180314

Published by Packt Publishing Ltd.
Livery Place
35 Livery Street
Birmingham B3 2PB, UK.

ISBN 978-1-78328-719-2

www.packtpub.com

Cover Image by Suman Kumar (sumankumarsinha@yahoo.com)

Credits

Author
Sébastien Armand

Reviewers
Vincent Composieux
Boris Guéry
Eric Pidoux
Adam Prager

Acquisition Editors
Rebecca Pedley
Antony Lowe

Content Development Editor
Rebecca Pedley

Technical Editors
Menza Mathew
Shali Sasidharan

Copy Editors
Alfida Paiva
Karuna Narayanan

Project Coordinator
Jomin Varghese

Proofreaders
Simran Bhogal
Maria Gould

Indexers
Mariammal Chettiyar
Monica Ajmera Mehta

Graphics
Yuvraj Mannari

Production Coordinator
Manu Joseph

Cover Work
Manu Joseph

About the Author

Sébastien Armand is a software developer based in Beijing, China. He spent most of the past five years working with Symfony, building internal IT systems. He co-founded `mashupsports.com`, a social website for sports enthusiasts based on Symfony2. He contributed to Symfony and the Symfony documentation on many occasions.

I would like to thank my ever-loving and understanding wife for all her support. If it weren't for her, I would have never started this book. Thank you. I'll be home for breakfast from now on! Also my parents and sister for just being awesome. Of course, I also extend my thanks to the whole Symfony community. It feels great being a part of it!

About the Reviewers

Vincent Composieux is a French PHP developer based in Paris and working at Ekino. Previously, he worked for e-commerce companies and web agencies on multiple great web projects with high traffic.

He loves web technologies and frameworks and has experience in using Zend Framework, Magento, and now Symfony.

He has had great experience in Symfony because he has used it since the very first version and is actively involved in the Symfony community. He has even developed some bundles such as FeedBundle for managing the RSS and Atom feeds and some others. He is also a contributor on the Sonata bundles suite.

You can learn more about him and contact him on his personal website via `http://vincent.composieux.fr`.

Boris Guéry is the CTO of Azurgate SA. He is a French startup editor and has edited the well-known French mobile application: Se Coucher Moins Bête. He is also a proud member of The Big Brains Company. He has been active on the Web since 1997, and has been using computers since he was four; he likes beer as well as software architecture and best practices. He is passionate of R&D yet pragmatic. He works mainly in PHP using Symfony2, but still picks anything that does the job (Python, Bash, C, and Ruby). He has developed a real expertise in implementing scalable applications on high-load applications.

> I would like to thank all my friends, with a special mention to all the members of The Big Brains Company. My deep gratitude goes to my parents as well.

Eric Pidoux has a master's degree in Computer Science from Miage Aix-Marseille and is currently working as a Lead Web Developer at Createur.ch (Lausanne, Switzerland), working especially on Symfony2 framework and PHP5 websites.

He started working as a Java and PHP developer and dropped the Java skill to learn Symfony and then become a Symfony2 expert.

He already worked as a technical reviewer on *GitLab Repository Management*, *J.M. Hethey*, *Packt Publishing*.

Adam Prager is a full stack web application developer who has created many data-heavy business management applications in the areas of Customer Relationship Management, Enterprise Resource Planning, and Laboratory Information Management.

He is a firm believer in the value and power of open source software, and contributes to projects such as Doctrine and Symfony regularly on GitHub. He has published numerous Symfony bundles and jQuery plugins of his own. Adam currently works for Netlife in Hungary.

Netlife is a consulting and IT services company that provides web application development services using the latest technologies, and complete business solutions based on SAP consulting.

As a diverse end-to-end IT solutions provider, Netlife offers a range of expertise aimed at assisting customers to compete successfully in the ever-changing IT industry. It provides long-term solutions with a focus on quality. They have excellent domain expertise in SAP CRM, custom web application development, and user experience design.

www.PacktPub.com

Support files, eBooks, discount offers, and more

You might want to visit www.PacktPub.com for support files and downloads related to your book.

Did you know that Packt offers eBook versions of every book published, with PDF and ePub files available? You can upgrade to the eBook version at www.PacktPub.com and as a print book customer, you are entitled to a discount on the eBook copy. Get in touch with us at service@packtpub.com for more details.

At www.PacktPub.com, you can also read a collection of free technical articles, sign up for a range of free newsletters and receive exclusive discounts and offers on Packt books and eBooks.

http://PacktLib.PacktPub.com

Do you need instant solutions to your IT questions? PacktLib is Packt's online digital book library. Here, you can access, read and search across Packt's entire library of books.

Why subscribe?

- Fully searchable across every book published by Packt
- Copy and paste, print and bookmark content
- On demand and accessible via web browser

Free access for Packt account holders

If you have an account with Packt at www.PacktPub.com, you can use this to access PacktLib today and view nine entirely free books. Simply use your login credentials for immediate access.

Table of Contents

Preface

The first stable version of Symfony2 was released more than two years back. Coming from all the experience acquired from Symfony1, the promise was to remove all the magic and provide a solid and modular basis to build web applications. The trade-off's inconvenience was justified in order for developers to regain full control and knowledge of the working of their application. To achieve this, it was decided that everything would be a bundle. The core framework itself is just a collection of bundles, which is everything you need to get started.

This great architecture being at the heart of Symfony2 and the promise of greater modularity and control over the whole framework enables any developer to create their own extensions. It is easy to implement these extensions; everything is prepared so that these extensions can be shared and their configuration can be disclosed for other developers to use them.

From the basics of creating a simple service to a custom authentication, this book will guide you through everything you need to create amazing bundles for Symfony2 and share them with the community.

What this book covers

Chapter 1, Services and Listeners, talks about the services and listeners that are the basis of nearly all extension techniques used in Symfony. This covers the fundamentals that will be reused throughout the book.

Chapter 2, Commands and Templates, helps you make your templates smarter and augment them with your own tailored functions and filters. This chapter helps you wrap common actions in commands so that you can perform them easily and reliably.

Chapter 3, Forms, helps you create your own form types and widgets and use them inside of dynamic forms that change based on the user information or even their own input.

Chapter 4, Security, discusses how to write custom authentication methods, use voters to restrict access, and add additional security layers to Symfony2.

Chapter 5, Doctrine, describes how to make your database fit your data and not the opposite. This chapter also describes how to write custom database types and extend Doctrine to easily share common domain logic between models.

Chapter 6, Sharing Your Extensions, helps you to create a great extension that others could benefit from. It contains everything you need to know about publishing a self-contained reusable bundle.

What you need for this book

You will need a working Symfony environment behind a web server (Apache, Nginx, and so on) and a relational database server such as MySQL or PostgreSQL. Some examples are based on using MongoDB but can be applied to other databases as well.

The book makes use of features available in Symfony 2.3 and higher. The examples might have to be adapted a bit if you are using an older version.

Some code also makes use of features available only in PHP 5.4 or higher, so they will need to be adapted to work with older versions of PHP.

Who this book is for

This book is for you if you fulfill the following conditions:

- You are already using Symfony2 and PHP
- You want to understand more about how it works under the hood
- You need to replicate some of the Symfony2 core features but ones that are tailored to your specific needs
- Your controllers and models are growing out of control
- You need a better way to structure and organize your application logic and code

This book is not for you if you are just getting started with Symfony2. It will confuse you more than it will help you. Keep it on your night stand for a while and come back to it later.

Conventions

In this book, you will find a number of styles of text that distinguish between different kinds of information. Here are some examples of these styles and an explanation of their meaning.

Code words in text are shown as follows: "The `php app/console container:debug <service_name>` command will provide information about a specific service."

A block of code is set as follows:

```
use Geocoder\HttpAdapter\CurlHttpAdapter;
use Geocoder\Geocoder;
use Geocoder\Provider\FreeGeoIpProvider;

public function indexAction()
  {
```

New terms and **important words** are shown in bold. Words that you see on the screen, in menus or dialog boxes for example, appear in the text like this: "If you have enabled colored output in your console, the line saying **Success!** should appear in green."

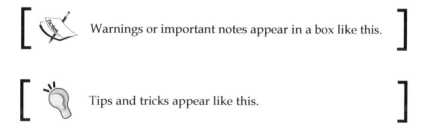

> Warnings or important notes appear in a box like this.

> Tips and tricks appear like this.

Reader feedback

Feedback from our readers is always welcome. Let us know what you think about this book—what you liked or may have disliked. Reader feedback is important for us to develop titles that you really get the most out of.

To send us general feedback, simply send an e-mail to `feedback@packtpub.com`, and mention the book title via the subject of your message.

If there is a topic that you have expertise in and you are interested in either writing or contributing to a book, see our author guide on `www.packtpub.com/authors`.

Customer support

Now that you are the proud owner of a Packt book, we have a number of things to help you to get the most from your purchase.

Downloading the example code

You can download the example code files for all Packt books you have purchased from your account at http://www.packtpub.com. If you purchased this book elsewhere, you can visit http://www.packtpub.com/support and register to have the files e-mailed directly to you.

Errata

Although we have taken every care to ensure the accuracy of our content, mistakes do happen. If you find a mistake in one of our books—maybe a mistake in the text or the code—we would be grateful if you would report this to us. By doing so, you can save other readers from frustration and help us improve subsequent versions of this book. If you find any errata, please report them by visiting http://www.packtpub.com/submit-errata, selecting your book, clicking on the **errata submission form** link, and entering the details of your errata. Once your errata are verified, your submission will be accepted and the errata will be uploaded on our website, or added to any list of existing errata, under the Errata section of that title. Any existing errata can be viewed by selecting your title from http://www.packtpub.com/support.

Piracy

Piracy of copyright material on the Internet is an ongoing problem across all media. At Packt, we take the protection of our copyright and licenses very seriously. If you come across any illegal copies of our works, in any form, on the Internet, please provide us with the location address or website name immediately so that we can pursue a remedy.

Please contact us at copyright@packtpub.com with a link to the suspected pirated material.

We appreciate your help in protecting our authors, and our ability to bring you valuable content.

Questions

You can contact us at questions@packtpub.com if you are having a problem with any aspect of the book, and we will do our best to address it.

1
Services and Listeners

This chapter will explain the basis of services in the Symfony2 framework. A **service** is an essential and core concept in Symfony2. In fact, most of the framework itself is just a big set of predefined services that are ready to use. As an example, if you just set up a new installation of Symfony2, from your project root, you can type `php app/console container:debug` to see the full list of services currently defined in your application. As you can see, even before we start writing anything for our application, we already have almost 200 services defined. The `php app/console container:debug <service_name>` command will provide information about a specific service and will be a useful command to refer to throughout the book.

Services

A service is just a specific instance of a given class. For example, whenever you access `doctrine` such as `$this->get('doctrine');` in a controller, it implies that you are accessing a service. This service is an instance of the `Doctrine EntityManager` class, but you never have to create this instance yourself. The code needed to create this entity manager is actually not that simple since it requires a connection to the database, some other configurations, and so on. Without this service already being defined, you would have to create this instance in your own code. Maybe you will have to repeat this initialization in each controller, thus making your application messier and harder to maintain.

Some of the default services present in Symfony2 are as follows:

- The annotation reader
- Assetic—the asset management library
- The event dispatcher
- The form widgets and form factory

- The Symfony2 Kernel and HttpKernel
- Monolog—the logging library
- The router
- Twig—the templating engine

It is very easy to create new services because of the Symfony2 framework. If we have a controller that has started to become quite messy with long code, a good way to refactor it and make it simpler will be to move some of the code to services. We have described all these services starting with "the" and a singular noun. This is because most of the time, services will be singleton objects where a single instance is needed.

A geolocation service

In this example, we imagine an application for listing events, which we will call "meetups". The controller makes it so that we can first retrieve the current user's IP address, use it as basic information to retrieve the user's location, and only display meetups within 50 kms of distance to the user's current location. Currently, the code is all set up in the controller. As it is, the controller is not actually that long yet, it has a single method and the whole class is around 50 lines of code. However, when you start to add more code, to only list the type of meetups that are the user's favorites or the ones they attended the most. When you want to mix that information and have complex calculations as to which meetups might be the most relevant to this specific user, the code could easily grow out of control!

There are many ways to refactor this simple example. The geocoding logic can just be put in a separate method for now, and this will be a good step, but let's plan for the future and move some of the logic to the services where it belongs. Our current code is as follows:

```
use Geocoder\HttpAdapter\CurlHttpAdapter;
use Geocoder\Geocoder;
use Geocoder\Provider\FreeGeoIpProvider;

public function indexAction()
  {
```

Initialize our geocoding tools (based on the excellent geocoding library at http://geocoder-php.org/) using the following code:

```
$adapter = new CurlHttpAdapter();
$geocoder = new Geocoder();
$geocoder->registerProviders(array(
  new FreeGeoIpProvider($adapter),
));
```

Retrieve our user's IP address using the following code:

```
$ip = $this->get('request')->getClientIp();
// Or use a default one
if ($ip == '127.0.0.1') {
  $ip = '114.247.144.250';
}
```

Get the coordinates and adapt them using the following code so that they are roughly a square of 50 kms on each side:

```
$result = $geocoder->geocode($ip);
$lat = $result->getLatitude();
$long = $result->getLongitude();
$lat_max = $lat + 0.25; // (Roughly 25km)
$lat_min = $lat - 0.25;
$long_max = $long + 0.3; // (Roughly 25km)
$long_min = $long - 0.3;
```

Create a query based on all this information using the following code:

```
$em = $this->getDoctrine()->getManager();
$qb = $em->createQueryBuilder();
$qb->select('e')
    ->from('KhepinBookBundle:Meetup, 'e')
    ->where('e.latitude < :lat_max')
    ->andWhere('e.latitude > :lat_min')
    ->andWhere('e.longitude < :long_max')
    ->andWhere('e.longitude > :long_min')
    ->setParameters([
      'lat_max' => $lat_max,
      'lat_min' => $lat_min,
      'long_max' => $long_max,
      'long_min' => $long_min
    ]);
```

Retrieve the results and pass them to the template using the following code:

```
$meetups = $qb->getQuery()->execute();
return ['ip' => $ip, 'result' => $result,
  'meetups' => $meetups];
}
```

The first thing we want to do is get rid of the geocoding initialization. It would be great to have all of this taken care of automatically and we would just access the geocoder with: `$this->get('geocoder');`.

You can define your services directly in the `config.yml` file of Symfony under the `services` key, as follows:

```
services:
    geocoder:
        class: Geocoder\Geocoder
```

That is it! We defined a service that can now be accessed in any of our controllers. Our code now looks as follows:

```
// Create the geocoding class
$adapter = new \Geocoder\HttpAdapter\CurlHttpAdapter();
$geocoder = $this->get('geocoder');
$geocoder->registerProviders(array(
    new \Geocoder\Provider\FreeGeoIpProvider($adapter),
));
```

Well, I can see you rolling your eyes, thinking that it is not really helping so far. That's because initializing the geocoder is a bit more complex than just using the `new \Geocoder\Geocoder()` code. It needs another class to be instantiated and then passed as a parameter to a method. The good news is that we can do all of this in our service definition by modifying it as follows:

```
services:
    # Defines the adapter class
    geocoder_adapter:
        class: Geocoder\HttpAdapter\CurlHttpAdapter
        public: false
    # Defines the provider class
    geocoder_provider:
        class: Geocoder\Provider\FreeGeoIpProvider
        public: false
        # The provider class is passed the adapter as an argument
        arguments: [@geocoder_adapter]
    geocoder:
        class: Geocoder\Geocoder
```

```
# We call a method on the geocoder after initialization to
  set up the
# right parameters
calls:
    - [registerProviders, [[@geocoder_provider]]]
```

It's a bit longer than this, but it is the code that we never have to write anywhere else ever again. A few things to notice are as follows:

- We actually defined three services, as our geocoder requires two other classes to be instantiated.

- We used `@+service_name` to pass a reference to a service as an argument to another service.

- We can do more than just defining `new Class($argument);` we can also call a method on the class after it is instantiated. It is even possible to set properties directly when they are declared as `public`.

- We marked the first two services as `private`. This means that they won't be accessible in our controllers. They can, however, be used by the **Dependency Injection Container (DIC)** to be injected into other services.

Our code now looks as follows:

```
// Retrieve current user's IP address
$ip = $this->get('request')->getClientIp();

// Or use a default one
if ($ip == '127.0.0.1') {
    $ip = '114.247.144.250';
}
// Find the user's coordinates
$result = $this->get('geocoder')->geocode($ip);
$lat = $result->getLatitude();
// ... Remaining code is unchanged
```

> Here, our controllers are extending the `BaseController` class, which has access to DIC since it implements the `ContainerAware` interface. All calls to `$this->get('service_name')` are proxied to the container that constructs (if needed) and returns the service.

Let's go one step further and define our own class that will directly get the user's IP address and return an array of maximum and minimum longitude and latitudes. We will create the following class:

```php
namespace Khepin\BookBundle\Geo;

use Geocoder\Geocoder;
use Symfony\Component\HttpFoundation\Request;

class UserLocator {

    protected $geocoder;

    protected $user_ip;

    public function __construct(Geocoder $geocoder, Request
      $request) {
        $this->geocoder = $geocoder;
        $this->user_ip = $request->getClientIp();
        if ($this->user_ip == '127.0.0.1') {
            $this->user_ip = '114.247.144.250';
        }
    }

    public function getUserGeoBoundaries($precision = 0.3) {
        // Find the user's coordinates
        $result = $this->geocoder->geocode($this->user_ip);
        $lat = $result->getLatitude();
        $long = $result->getLongitude();
        $lat_max = $lat + 0.25; // (Roughly 25km)
        $lat_min = $lat - 0.25;
        $long_max = $long + 0.3; // (Roughly 25km)
        $long_min = $long - 0.3;
        return ['lat_max' => $lat_max, 'lat_min' => $lat_min,
            'long_max' => $long_max, 'long_min' => $long_min];
    }
}
```

It takes our geocoder and request variables as arguments, and then does all the heavy work we were doing in the controller at the beginning of the chapter. Just as we did before, we will define this class as a service, as follows, so that it becomes very easy to access from within the controllers:

```yaml
# config.yml
services:
    #...
```

```
user_locator:
    class: Khepin\BookBundle\Geo\UserLocator
    scope: request
    arguments: [@geocoder, @request]
```

Notice that we have defined the scope here. The DIC has two scopes by default: `container` and `prototype`, to which the framework also adds a third one named `request`. The following table shows their differences:

Scope	Differences
Container	All calls to `$this->get('service_name')` return the same instance of the service.
Prototype	Each call to `$this->get('service_name')` returns a new instance of the service.
Request	Each call to `$this->get('service_name')` returns the same instance of the service within a request. Symfony can have subrequests (such as including a controller in Twig).

Now, the advantage is that the service knows everything it needs by itself, but it also becomes unusable in contexts where there are no requests. If we wanted to create a command that gets all users' last-connected IP address and sends them a newsletter of the meetups around them on the weekend, this design would prevent us from using the `Khepin\BookBundle\Geo\UserLocator` class to do so.

As we see, by default, the services are in the container scope, which means they will only be instantiated once and then reused, therefore implementing the singleton pattern. It is also important to note that the DIC does not create all the services immediately, but only on demand. If your code in a different controller never tries to access the `user_locator` service, then that service and all the other ones it depends on (`geocoder`, `geocoder_provider`, and `geocoder_adapter`) will never be created.

Also, remember that the configuration from the `config.yml` is cached when on a production environment, so there is also little to no overhead in defining these services.

Our controller looks a lot simpler now and is as follows:

```
$boundaries = $this->get('user_locator')->getUserGeoBoundaries();
// Create our database query
$em = $this->getDoctrine()->getManager();
$qb = $em->createQueryBuilder();
$qb->select('e')
    ->from('KhepinBookBundle:Meetup', 'e')
```

```
            ->where('e.latitude < :lat_max')
            ->andWhere('e.latitude > :lat_min')
            ->andWhere('e.longitude < :long_max')
            ->andWhere('e.longitude > :long_min')
            ->setParameters($boundaries);
    // Retrieve interesting meetups
    $meetups = $qb->getQuery()->execute();
    return ['meetups' => $meetups];
```

The longest part here is the doctrine query, which we could easily put on the
repository class to further simplify our controller.

As we just saw, defining and creating services in Symfony2 is fairly easy and
inexpensive. We created our own `UserLocator` class, made it a service, and saw that
it can depend on our other services such as `@geocoder` service. We are not finished
with services or the DIC as they are the underlying part of almost everything related
to extending Symfony2. We will keep seeing them throughout this book; therefore,
it is important to have a good understanding of them before continuing.

Testing services and testing with services

One of the great advantages of putting your code in a service is that a service is just
a simple PHP class. This makes it very easy to unit test. You don't actually need the
controller or the DIC. All you need is to create mocks of a `geocoder` and `request` class.

In the `test` folder of the bundle, we can add a `Geo` folder where we test our
`UserLocator` class. Since we are only testing a simple PHP class, we don't need
to use `WebTestCase`. The standard `PHPUnit_Framework_TestCase` will suffice.
Our class has only one method that geocodes an IP address and returns a set of
coordinates based on the required precision. We can mock the geocoder to return
fixed numbers and therefore avoid a network call that would slow down our tests.
A simple test case looks as follows:

```
class UserLocatorTest extends PHPUnit_Framework_TestCase
{
    public function testGetBoundaries()
    {
        $geocoder = $this->getMock('Geocoder\Geocoder');
        $result = $this->getMock('Geocoder\Result\Geocoded');

        $geocoder->expects($this->any())->method('geocode')-
            >will($this->returnValue($result));
        $result->expects($this->any())->method('getLatitude')-
            >will($this->returnValue(3));
```

```
$result->expects($this->any())->method('getLongitude')
  ->will($this->returnValue(7));

$request = $this->getMock
  ('Symfony\Component\HttpFoundation\Request',
    ['getUserIp']);
$locator = new UserLocator($geocoder, $request);

$boundaries = $locator->getUserGeoBoundaries(0);

$this->assertTrue($boundaries['lat_min'] == 3);
        }
    }
```

We can now simply verify that our class itself is working, but what about the whole controller logic?

We can write a simple integration test for this controller and test for the presence and absence of some meetups on the rendered page. However, in some cases, for performance, convenience, or because it is simply not possible, we don't want to actually call the external services while testing. In that case, it is also possible to mock the services that will be used in the controller. In your tests, you will need to do the following:

```
public function testIndexMock()
{
    $client = static::createClient();
    $locator = $this->getMockBuilder
      ('Khepin\BookBundle\Geo\UserLocator')
        ->disableOriginalConstructor()->getMock();
    $boundaries = ["lat_max" => 40.2289, "lat_min" => 39.6289,
      "long_max" => 116.6883, "long_min" => 116.0883];
    $locator->expects($this->any())->method
      ('getUserGeoBoundaries')->will($this-
        >returnValue($boundaries));
    $client->getContainer()->set('user_locator', $locator);
    $crawler = $client->request('GET', '/');
  // Verify that the page contains the meetups we expect

}
```

Here, we mock the UserLocator class so that it will always return the same coordinates. This way, we can better control what we are testing and avoid waiting for a long call to the geolocation server.

Tagging services

You have most likely already encountered tagged services when using Symfony, for example, if you have defined custom form widgets or security voters. Event listeners, which we will talk about in the second part of this chapter, are also tagged services.

In our previous examples, we created a `user_locator` service that relies on a geocoder service. However, there are many possible ways to locate a user. We can have their address information in their profile, which will be faster and more accurate than getting it from a user's IP address. We can use different online providers such as FreeGeoIp as we did in the previous code, or have a local `geoip` database. We can even have all of these in our application at the same time, and try them one after the other from most to least accurate.

Let's define the interface for this new type of geocoder as follows:

```
namespace Khepin\BookBundle\Geo;

interface Geocoder
{
    public function getAccuracy();

    public function geocode($ip);
}
```

We will then define two geocoders using the following code; the first one just wraps our existing one in a new class that implements our `Geocoder` interface:

```
namespace Khepin\BookBundle\Geo;
use Geocoder\Geocoder as IpGeocoder;

class FreeGeoIpGeocoder implements Geocoder
{
    public function __construct(IpGeocoder $geocoder)
    {
        $this->geocoder = $geocoder;
    }

    public function geocode($ip)
    {
        return $this->geocoder->geocode($ip);
    }

    public function getAccuracy()
    {
        return 100;
    }
}
```

The first type of geocoder is configured as follows:

```
freegeoip_geocoder:
    class: Khepin\BookBundle\Geo\FreeGeoIpGeocoder
    arguments: [@geocoder]
```

The second geocoder returns a random location every time, as follows:

```
namespace Khepin\BookBundle\Geo;

class RandomLocationGeocoder implements Geocoder
{
    public function geocode($ip)
    {
        return new Result();
    }

    public function getAccuracy()
    {
        return 0;
    }
}

class Result
{
    public function getLatitude()
    {
        return rand(-85, 85);
    }

    public function getLongitude()
    {
        return rand(-180, 180);
    }

    public function getCountryCode()
    {
        return 'CN';
    }
}
```

The second geocoder is configured as follows:

```
random_geocoder:
    class: Khepin\BookBundle\Geo\RandomLocationGeocoder
```

Now, if we change the configuration of our `user_locator` service to use any of these geocoders, things will work correctly. However, what we really want is that it has access to all the available geolocation methods and then picks the most accurate one, even when we add new ones without changing the `user_locator` service.

Let's tag our services by modifying their configuration to add a tag as follows:

```
freegeoip_geocoder:
    class: Khepin\BookBundle\Geo\FreeGeoIpGeocoder
    arguments: [@geocoder]
    tags:
        - { name: khepin_book.geocoder }
random_geocoder:
    class: Khepin\BookBundle\Geo\RandomLocationGeocoder
    tags:
        - { name: khepin_book.geocoder }
```

We cannot pass all of these in the constructor of our class directly, so we'll modify our `UserLocator` class to have an `addGeocoder` method as follows:

```
class UserLocator
{    protected $geocoders = [];

    protected $user_ip;

    // Removed the geocoder from here
    public function __construct(Request $request)
    {
        $this->user_ip = $request->getClientIp();
    }

    public function addGeocoder(Geocoder $geocoder)
    {
        $this->geocoders[] = $geocoder;
    }

    // Picks the most accurate geocoder
    public function getBestGeocoder(){/* ... */}

    // ...
}
```

Informing the DIC that we want to add tagged services cannot be done only through configuration. This is instead done through a compiler pass when the DIC is being compiled.

Compiler passes allow you to dynamically modify service definitions. They can be used for tagged services and for creating bundles that enable extra functionalities whenever another bundle is also present and configured. The compiler pass can be used as follows:

```
namespace Khepin\BookBundle\DependencyInjection\Compiler;

use Symfony\Component\DependencyInjection\ContainerBuilder;
use Symfony\Component\DependencyInjection\Compiler
  \CompilerPassInterface;
use Symfony\Component\DependencyInjection\Reference;

class UserLocatorPass implements CompilerPassInterface
{
    public function process(ContainerBuilder $container)
    {
      if (!$container->hasDefinition('khepin_book.user_locator'))
        {
            return;
        }

        $service_definition = $container->getDefinition
          ('khepin_book.user_locator');
        $tagged = $container->findTaggedServiceIds
        ('khepin_book.geocoder');

        foreach ($tagged as $id => $attrs) {
            $service_definition->addMethodCall(
              'addGeocoder',
              [new Reference($id)]
            );
        }
    }
}
```

After we have confirmed that the `user_locator` (renamed here as `khepin_book.user_locator`) service exists, we find all the services with the corresponding tag and modify the service definition for `khepin_book.user_locator` so that it loads these services.

> You can define custom attributes on a tag. So, we could have moved the accuracy of each geocoder to the configuration as follows, and then used the compiler pass to only provide the most accurate geocoder to the user locator:
>
> ```
> tags:
>         - { name: khepin_book.geocoder, accuracy: 69 }
> ```

Whenever we define the YAML configuration for services, Symfony will internally create service definitions based on that information. By adding a compiler pass, we can modify these service definitions dynamically. The service definitions are then all cached so that we don't have to compile the container again.

Listeners

Listeners are a way of implementing the observer's design pattern. In this pattern, a particular piece of code does not try to start the execution of all the code that should happen at a given time. Instead, it notifies all of its observers that it has reached a given point in execution and lets these observers to take over the control flow if they have to.

In Symfony, we use the observer's pattern through events. Any class or function can trigger an event whenever it sees the event fit. The event itself can be defined in a class. This allows the passing of more information to the code observing this event. The framework itself will trigger events at different points in the process of handling the requests. These events are as follows:

- `kernel.request`: This event happens before reaching a controller. It is used internally to populate the `request` object.

- `kernel.controller`: This event happens immediately before executing the controller. It can be used to change the controller being executed.

- `kernel.view`: This event happens after executing the controller and if the controller did not return a `response` object. For example, this will be used to let Twig handle the rendering of a view by default.

- `kernel.response`: This event happens before the response is sent out. It can be used to modify the response before it is sent out.

- `kernel.terminate`: This event happens after the response has been sent out. It can be used to perform any time-consuming operations that are not necessary to generate the response.

- `kernel.exception`: This event happens whenever the framework catches an exception that was not handled.

> Doctrine will also trigger events during an object's lifecycle (such as before or after persisting it to the database), but they are a whole different topic. You can learn everything about **Doctrine LifeCycle Events** at `http://docs.doctrine-project.org/en/latest/reference/events.html`.

Events are very powerful and we will use them in many places throughout this book. When you begin sharing your Symfony extensions with others, it is *always* a good idea to define and trigger custom events as these can be used as your own extension points.

We will build on the example provided in the *Services* section to see what use we could make of the listeners.

In the first part, we made our site that only shows a user the meetups that are happening around him or her. We now want to show meetups also taking into account a user's preferences (most joined meetups).

We have updated the schema to have a many-to-many relationship between users and the meetups as follows:

```
// Entity/User.php
/**
 * @ORM\ManyToMany(targetEntity="Meetup", mappedBy="attendees")
 */
protected $meetups;

// Entity/Meetup.php
/**
 * @ORM\ManyToMany(targetEntity="User", inversedBy="meetups")
 */
protected $attendees;
```

In our controller, we have a simple action to join a meetup, which is as follows:

```
/**
 * @Route("/meetups/{meetup_id}/join")
 * @Template()
 */
public function joinAction($meetup_id) {
    $em = $this->getDoctrine()->getManager();
    $meetup = $em->getRepository('KhepinBookBundle:Meetup')
      ->find($meetup_id);

    $form = $this->createForm(
      new JoinMeetupType(),
      $meetup,
      ['action' => '', 'method' => 'POST']
    );
    $form->add('submit', 'submit', array('label' => 'Join'));
```

```
$form->handleRequest($this->get('request'));

$user = $this->get('security.context')->getToken()->getUser();

if ($form->isValid()) {
    $meetup->addAttendee($user);
    $em->flush();
}

$form = $form->createView();
return ['meetup' => $meetup, 'user' => $user,
    'form' => $form];
}
```

We use a form even for such a simple action because getting all
our information from the URL in order to update the database and
register this user as an attendee would enable many vulnerability
issues such as CSRF attacks.

Updating user preferences using custom events

We want to add some code to generate the new list of favorite meetups of our user.
This will allow us to change the logic for displaying the frontpage. Now, we can
not only show users all the meetups happening around them, but also data will
be filtered as to how likely they are to enjoy this kind of meetup. Our users will
view the frontpage often, making the cost of calculating their favorite meetups on
each page load very high. Therefore, we prefer to have a pre-calculated list of their
favorite meetup types. We will update this list whenever a user joins or resigns
from a meetup. In the future, we can also update it based on the pages they browse,
even without actually joining the meetup.

The problem now is to decide where this code should live. The easy and immediate
answer could be to add it right here in our controller. But, we can see that this logic
doesn't really belong here. The controller makes sure that a user can join a meetup.
It should limit its own logic to just doing that.

What is possible though is to let the controller call an event, warning all observers
that a user has joined a meetup and letting these observers decide what is best to do
with this information.

For this event to be useful, it needs to hold information about the user and the meetup. Let's create a simple class using the following code to hold that information:

```
// Bundle/Event/MeetupEvent.php
namespace Khepin\BookBundle\Event;

use Symfony\Component\EventDispatcher\Event;
use Khepin\BookBundle\Entity\User;
use Khepin\BookBundle\Entity\Meetup;

class MeetupEvent extends Event
{
    protected $user;
    protected $event;

    public function __construct(User $user, Meetup $meetup) {
        $this->user = $user;
        $this->meetup= $meetup;
    }

    public function getUser() {
        return $this->user;
    }

    public function getMeetup() {
        return $this->meetup;
    }
}
```

This class is very simple and is only here to hold data about an event regarding a meetup and a user. Now let's trigger that event whenever a user joins a meetup. In our controller, use the following code after validating the form:

```
if ($form->isValid()) {
    $meetup->addAttendee($user);
    // This is the new line
    $this->get('event_dispatcher')->dispatch(
      'meetup.join',
      new MeetupEvent($user, $meetup)
    );
    $em->flush();
}
```

All we did was find the `event_dispatcher` service and dispatch the `meetup.join` event associated with some data. Dispatching an event is nothing more than just sending a message under a name, `meetup.join` in our case, potentially with some data. Before the code keeps on executing to the next line, all the classes and objects that listen to that event will be given the opportunity to run some code as well.

> It is a good practice to namespace your events to avoid event name collisions. The dot (.) notation is usually preferred to separate event namespaces. So, it's very common to find events such as `acme.user.authentication.success`, `acme.user.authentication.fail`, and so on.

Another good practice is to catalog and document your events. We can see that if we keep on adding many events, since they are so easy to trigger because it's only a name, we will have a hard time keeping track of what events we have and what their purpose is. It is even more important to catalog your events if you intend to share your code with other people at some point. To do that, we create a static events class as follows:

```
namespace Khepin\BookBundle\Event;

final class MeetupEvents
{
    /**
     * The meetup.join event is triggered every time a user
     * registers for a meetup.
     *
     * Listeners receive an instance of:
     * Khepin\BookBundle\Event\MeetupEvent
     */
    const MEETUP_JOIN = 'meetup.join';
}
```

As we said, this class is much more for documentation purposes than anything else. Your code can now be changed in the controller as follows:

```
$container->get('event_dispatcher')->dispatch(
    MeetupEvents::MEETUP_JOIN,
    new MeetupEvent($user, $meetup)
);
```

We now know how to trigger an event, but we can't say that it has helped us to achieve anything interesting so far! Let's add a little bit of logic based on that. We will first create a listener class using the following code that will be responsible for generating the user's new list of preferred meetups:

```
namespace Khepin\BookBundle\Event\Listener;
use Khepin\BookBundle\Event\MeetupEvent;

class JoinMeetupListener
{
    public function generatePreferences(MeetupEvent $event) {
        $user = $event->getUser();
        $meetup = $event->getMeetup();
        // Logic to generate the user's new preferences
    }
}
```

Our class is a plain PHP class; it doesn't need to extend anything special. Therefore, it doesn't need to have any specific name. All it needs is to have at least one method that accepts a MeetupEvent argument. If we were to execute the code now, nothing would happen as we never said that this class should listen to a specific event. This is done by making this class a service again. This means that our listener could also be passed an instance of our geolocation service that we defined in the first part of this chapter, or any other existing Symfony service. The definition of our listener as a service, however, shows us some more advanced use of services:

```
join_meetup_listener:
    class: Khepin\BookBundle\Event\Listener\JoinMeetupListener
    tags:
        - { name: kernel.event_listener, event: meetup.join,
          method: generatePreferences }
```

What the tags section means is that when the event_dispatcher service is first created, it will also look for other services that were given a specific tag (kernel. event_listener in this case) and remember them. This is used by other Symfony components too, such as the form framework (which we'll see in *Chapter 3, Forms*).

Improving user performance

We have achieved something great by using events and listeners. All the logic related to calculating a user's meetup preferences is now isolated in its own listener class. We didn't detail the implementation of that logic, but we already know from this chapter that it would be a good idea to not keep it in the controller, but as an independent service that could be called from the listener. The more you use Symfony, the more this idea will seem clear and obvious; all the code that can be moved to a service should be moved to a service. Some Symfony core developers even advocate that controllers themselves should be services. Following this practice will make your code simpler and more testable.

Code that works after the response

Now, when our site grows in complexity and usage, our calculation of users' preferred event types could take quite a while. Maybe the users can now have friends on our site, and we want a user's choice to also affect his or her friend's preferences.

There are many cases in modern web applications where very long operations are not essential in order to return a response to the user. Some of the cases are as follows:

- After uploading a video, a user shouldn't wait until the conversion of the video to another format is finished before seeing a page that tells him or her that the upload was successful

- A few seconds could maybe be saved if we don't resize the user's profile picture before showing that the update went through

- In our case, the user shouldn't wait until we have propagated to all his or her friends the news of him or her joining a meetup, to see that he or she is now accepted and taking part in the meetup

There are many ways to deal with such situations and to remove unnecessary work from the process of generating a response. You can use batch processes that will recalculate all user preferences every day, but this will cause a lag in response time as the updates will be only once a day, and can be a waste of resources. You can also use a setup with a message queue and workers, where the queue notifies the workers that they should do something. This is somewhat similar to what we just did with events, but the code taking care of the calculation will now run in a different process, or maybe even on a different machine. Also, we won't wait for it to complete in order to proceed.

Symfony offers a simple way to achieve this while keeping everything inside the framework. By listening to the `kernel.terminate` event, we can run our listener's method after the response has been sent to the client.

We will update our code to take advantage of this. Our new listener will now behave as explained in the following table:

Event	Listener
meetup.join	Remembers the user and meetup involved for later use. No calculation happens.
kernel.terminate	Actually generates the user preferences. The heavy calculation takes place.

Our code should then look as follows:

```
class JoinMeetupListener
{
    protected $event;

    public function onUserJoinsMeetup(MeetupEvent $event) {
        $this->event = $event;
    }

    public function generatePreferences() {
        if ($this->event) {
            // Generate the new preferences for the user
        }
    }
}
```

We then need to also update the configuration to call generatePreferences on the kernel.terminate event, as follows:

```
join_meetup_listener:
        class: Khepin\BookBundle\Event\Listener\JoinMeetupListener
        tags:
            - { name: kernel.event_listener, event: meetup.join,
              method: onUserJoinsMeetup }
            - { name: kernel.event_listener, event:
              kernel.terminate, method: generatePreferences }
```

This is done very simply by only adding a tag to our existing listener. If you were thinking about creating a new service of the same class but listening on a different event, you will have two different instances of the service. So, the service that remembered the event will never be called to generate the preferences, and the service called to generate the preferences will never have an event to work with. Through this new setup, our heavy calculation code is now out of the way for sending a response to the user, and he or she can now enjoy a faster browsing experience.

Summary

This chapter introduced two of the most important concepts in Symfony, especially when it comes to extending the framework. By creating our geocoding service, we saw how easy it is to add a service that is just like any of the other Symfony services. We also reviewed how to use events to keep your code logic where it belongs and avoid cluttering your controllers with unwanted code. Then finally, we used them to make your site faster and more responsive to your users.

Believe it or not, if you really understand services and events, you know almost everything about extending Symfony. You will see throughout this book that we will constantly keep referring to both of these concepts, so, it is important that you have a good understanding of them.

In the next chapter, we will augment Symfony by adding new commands to the console tool and customize the templating engine. We will see that the services can be really helpful there as well.

2
Commands and Templates

In this chapter, we will review two of the most common kinds of extensions that you will encounter while working on a Symfony project:

- **Commands**: They are similar to the ones that Symfony brings you, such as the ones already in the framework (`cache:clear`, `doctrine:database:create`, and so on)

- **Twig**: It's relatively easy to extend the templating language of Symfony as well

Commands

Symfony ships with a powerful console component. Just like many components in Symfony, it can also be used as a standalone component to create command-line programs. In fact, **Composer** (`http://getcomposer.org`), the dependency manager that you use every day with Symfony, has its command line-based on the Symfony Console component.

Let's find out how to create commands and what they are good for.

The initial situation

Our site users have a profile on the website. On their profile, they can upload their own picture (in any avatar). They can upload any kind of picture with different sizes and ratios, and the system will crop it and/or resize it to a square picture of 150 x 150 pixels. We always keep the higher resolution uploaded picture but pregenerate the 150-pixel one to improve the load speed of our site. Now that so many people are browsing our site from very high resolution tablets, we need to make that profile picture also available in 300 pixels size.

This is a relatively heavy task as it must apply to all of our users in one pass and involves image processing. This is also not something that should be available to our users, but only to the tech people; therefore, a controller doesn't seem like the right place for this functionality. Furthermore, this is probably a one-time thing, unless the process crashes in the middle or we need to have images of 600 pixels in a couple of months when even higher resolution displays appear! In this case, a Console command seems the appropriate place.

Resizing user pictures

We'll write our first command that just works on a single image and resizes it. To simplify the process of manipulating images, we will rely on the Imagine library (`https://imagine.readthedocs.org/en/latest/`). A command should extend the Symfony base command class. Within the framework, if you want to be able to use other services, it is easier to directly extend from Symfony. The two important functions in this class that you must define are `configure()` and `execute()`. Enter the following lines of code in the `configure()` function:

```
class ResizePictureCommand extends ContainerAwareCommand
{
    protected function configure()
    {
        $this
            ->setName('picture:resize')
            ->setDescription('Resize a single picture')
            ->addArgument('path', InputArgument::REQUIRED,'Path to
              the picture you want to resize')
            ->addOption('size', null, InputOption::VALUE_OPTIONAL,
              'Size of the output picture (default 300 pixels)')
            ->addOption('out', 'o', InputOption::VALUE_OPTIONAL,
              'Folder which to output the picture (default same as
                original picture)')
        ;

    }
```

In the preceding `configure()` function, we choose a command name, define the arguments (picture path), and some optional parameters. Now, our command can be invoked using the following command statement:

```
$./app/console picture:resize <path> (--size=) (--out|-o=)
```

Now, enter the following lines of code in the `execute()` function:

```
protected function execute(InputInterface $input,
    OutputInterface $output)
{
    // Command line info
    $path = $input->getArgument('path');
    $size = $input->getOption('size') ?: 300;
    $out = $input->getOption('out');

    // Prepare image and resize tool
    $imagine = new \Imagine\Gd\Imagine();
    $image = $imagine->open($path);
    $box = new \Imagine\Image\Box($size, $size);

    $filename = basename($path);

    // Resize image
    $image->resize($box)->save($out.'/'.$filename);

    $output->writeln(sprintf('%s --> %s', $path, $out));
}

}
```

In the `execute()` method, we receive an `$input` and `$output` argument representing the following:

- The command-line arguments we passed in as the input
- The console to which we can write information for the user

We get this information or replace it with the default ones using the Imagine image manipulation library and resize our picture. Finally, we output some information that tells us all went well.

Nothing extraordinary here, but this shows how we can create a simple command. Let's now try to apply that to all our users. We will create a command that browses through the list of our users and executes this command for each of them. To make things nice and simple, we won't ask the user to remember the order of arguments but display a series of questions on the console. We'll also add a progress bar, shown as follows, so the person using it knows how much is done or left to do:

```
class UpdateProfilePicsCommand extends ContainerAwareCommand
{
    protected function configure()
```

```
{
    $this
        ->setName('picture:profile:update')
        ->setDescription('Resizes all user\'s pictures to a new
            size');
}

protected function execute(InputInterface $input,
    OutputInterface $output)
{
    $dialog = $this
                    ->getHelperSet()
                    ->get('dialog');
    $size = $dialog->ask($output, 'Size of the final pictures
        (300): ', '300');
    $out = $dialog->ask($output, 'Output folder: ');
```

We use the dialog helper to display questions to the command-line user and get the necessary information.

```
    $command = $this->getApplication()->find('picture:resize');
    $arguments = array(
        'command' => 'picture:resize',
        '--size'  => $size,
        '--out'   => $out

    );
```

We get the command that we previously defined for resizing a single picture and prepare the arguments for calling the command. This is shown in the following code snippet:

```
// Get list of all users
$users = $this
                ->getContainer()->get('fos_user.user_manager')
                ->findUsers();
$progress = $this->getHelperSet()->get('progress');

$progress->start($output, count($users));
```

Here, we use the progress helper that we saw earlier and set its maximum value as the total number of users in our database. You don't need to calculate percentages by yourself; just provide the total number of unit steps that will be processed and the helper will do the rest.

```
foreach($users as $user) {
    // Run the picutre:resize command
```

```
        $arguments['path'] = $user->getPicture();
        $input = new ArrayInput($arguments);
        $command->run($input, $output);

        // Advance progress
        $progress->advance();
    }

    // Show that the whole process was successful
    $output->writeln('');
    $output->writeln('<info>Success!</info>');
    }

}
```

The output in our terminal should look like the following:

```
seb@seb ~/projects/extending-symfony/project $ ./console picture:profile:update
Size of the final pictures (300):
Output folder: web/pictures/resized
 1000/1000 [=============================] 100%
Success!
```

The command runs successfully, and if you have enabled colored output in your console, the line saying **Success!** should appear in green. We should now test our command to ensure it behaves correctly.

Testing a command

As with everything in our application, we would feel more confident knowing that there are tests that ensure it runs smoothly. We can see that our `picture:resize` command will be, in a way, hard to test. We cannot really mock anything it's going to use as it doesn't take any PHP objects as a parameter; it only takes input strings. It looks like we'll need to actually resize a picture to test it in its current stage. Let's try that using the following lines of code:

```
use Symfony\Bundle\FrameworkBundle\Console\Application as App;
use Symfony\Component\Console\Tester\CommandTester;
use Symfony\Bundle\FrameworkBundle\Test\WebTestCase;
use Khepin\BookBundle\Command\ResizePictureCommand;

class ResizePictureCommandTest extends WebTestCase
{
```

```php
public function testCommand()
{
    $kernel = $this->createKernel();
    $kernel->boot();

    $application = new App($kernel);
    $application->add(new ResizePictureCommand());

    $command = $application->find('picture:resize');
    $commandTester = new CommandTester($command);
    $commandTester->execute([
            'command' => $command->getName(),
            'path' => __DIR__.'/fixtures/pic.png',
            '-o' => __DIR__.'/fixtures/resized/'
        ]);

    $this
        ->assertTrue(file_exists(__DIR__.'/fixtures/
            resized/pic.png'));
}

}
```

It might seem weird to some of you that we extend this test class from `WebTestCase` and not from a standard `PHPUnit_Framework_TestCase`. This is mostly for convenience as the `WebTestCase` class gives us methods to directly access an initialized kernel. Otherwise, you would have to mock or create the kernel yourself.

To avoid messing with our whole application, we only test on a picture file that is inside our `test` folder in a `fixtures` subfolder.

Commands as an interface to services

We saw that our test is a bit special as it needs to actually resize a picture so that we can say it performed correctly. We can't pass it a mocked version of Imagine and check if the right calls to the library are made as we could have done if it were a service.

However, we saw that it is possible to call services from within a command, like when we used the `fos_user.user_manager` service to retrieve our list of users. We could, therefore, actually move all the core tasks performed by our command to a service and then have that command act only as an interface to input some arguments.

There are tremendous advantages in doing this, and we can only hope that more developers in the Symfony community start adopting this practice. It doesn't stop with testing. Opening a terminal is already a technical operation for many people. If this operation of resizing pictures becomes more frequent, why not have a web interface for starting the process that the site admins could use?

Loading fixture data in your database is something most developers would think of using, but again, you could benefit from having this defined as a service. It will be available from a controller when you want to prepopulate a new user's demo account.

I strongly encourage everyone to follow this practice of having very thin commands that are actually only an interface to something else. Let's do it right now and refactor our commands a bit.

We start with the `picture:resize` command and extract its logic to a service class.

```
namespace Khepin\BookBundle\Command;

class Shrinker
{
    protected $imagine;

    public function __construct($imagine)
    {
        $this->imagine = $imagine;
    }

    public function shrinkImage($path, $out, $size)
    {
        $image = $this->imagine->open($path);
        $box = new \Imagine\Image\Box($size, $size);
        $filename = basename($path);
        $image->resize($box)->save($out.'/'.$filename);
    }
}
```

The configuration for that new service is the following:

```
imagine:
    class: Imagine\Gd\Imagine
khepin_book.shrinker:
    class: Khepin\BookBundle\Command\Shrinker
    arguments: [@imagine]
```

Our command then becomes as follows:

```
$path = $input->getArgument('path');
$size = $input->getOption('size') ?: 300;
$out = $input->getOption('out');

$this->getContainer()->get('khepin_book.shrinker')->shrinkImage($path,
$out, $size);

$output->writeln(sprintf('%s --> %s', $path, $out));
```

As you can see, it is now only a very thin wrapper around our service. So thin indeed, that it starts feeling weird having all this complexity in our command that resizes all the user's pictures. It doesn't matter if we keep our command to resize only one picture; the `picture:profile:update` command directly calls the `shrinker` service. This is shown in the following code snippet:

```
protected function execute(InputInterface $input,
    OutputInterface $output)
{
    $dialog = $this->getHelperSet()->get('dialog');
    $size = $dialog->ask($output, 'Size of the final pictures
        (300): ', '300');
    $out = $dialog->ask($output, 'Output folder: ');

    // start shrinking
    $users = $this
                ->getContainer()
                ->get('fos_user.user_manager')->findUsers();

    $progress = $this->getHelperSet()->get('progress');
    $progress->start($output, count($users));

    foreach($users as $user) {
        $path = $user->getPicture();
        $this
            ->getContainer()
            ->get('khepin_book.shrinker')
            ->shrinkImage($path, $out, $size);

        // Advance progress
        $progress->advance();
    }
    // finish shrinking
```

```
    // Show that the whole process was successful
    $output->writeln('');
    $output->writeln('<info>Success!</info>');
}
```

As an added benefit, services are only created once and then reused. We no longer create an instance of Imagine for each picture resize or for one instance of the simple command. We always have access to the same one. In fact, we could again reduce the size of our command and move more logic to a service that would then be reusable. All the code between the `// start shrinking` and `// finish shrinking` comments should be as follows:

```
$this
    ->getContainer()
    ->get('khepin_book.user_manager')
    ->resizeAllPictures($size, $out);
```

If this service was sending events, as we saw in the previous chapter, you could still get the progress information, and it could now be used directly outside of a command.

Twig

By default, Symfony ships with the Twig templating system. Twig is incredibly powerful and out of the box. The possibilities offered by blocks, extending templates, including templates, and macros are huge and will be enough for most cases. There are cases where you still need something more though, and an extension for Twig is the only elegant way of doing so.

Twig offers five different ways to create extensions:

- **Globals**: This lets you define some global variables that are available in all templates. You could access them like any other variable.

- **Functions**: This will let you write `{{my_function(var)}}`.

- **Tests**: These are specific functions that return Boolean values and can be used after the `is` keyword in templates.

- **Filters**: They modify the output of an output tag.

- **Tags**: This will let you define custom Twig tags.

Some of the pages on our website will require some JavaScript in them to make them a bit more dynamic or simple to use. The form to create a meetup for organizers will definitely use a datepicker. The events page might display a map from Google or Bing's APIs. We are not creating a complete JavaScript application, just adding the bits we need here and there.

Managing our scripts

To improve the perceived page-load speed, it's usually good to load all our scripts at the end of the page. However, if we output the tag for the datepicker files to be loaded in the same template where we have the datepicker, things become more manageable. This is because when we decide to remove or change it, we don't need to remember it.

So, while rendering the templates, we'd prefer if there was a way to write a tag for the JavaScript to be loaded, but actually have the output of that tag be somewhere at the bottom of our generated HTML page. As Twig cannot deal with this, we'll create an extension for it.

```php
class KhepinExtension extends \Twig_Extension
{
    protected $javascripts = [];

    public function getFunctions()
    {
        return [
            new \Twig_SimpleFunction('jslater', [$this, 'jslater'])
            ];
    }

    public function jslater($src)
    {
        $this->javascripts[] = $src;
    }

    public function getName()
    {
        return 'khepin_extension';
    }

}
```

We start with this simple extension. It declares a Twig function that will remember the source path for any JavaScript tag that is passed to it. In our templates, we use it as follows:

```
{{jslater('web/scripts/datepicker.js')}}
```

We now need Twig to be aware of the existence of this extension. *How is this done?* You guessed it, by making our extension a service and giving it the proper tag. To do so, use the following lines of code:

```
khepin.twig.khepin_extension:
    class: Khepin\BookBundle\Twig\KhepinExtension
    tags:
        - { name: twig.extension }
```

The first part of our extension is working, so now we need to be able to output a `<script>` tag for each of the scripts that we collected using the following lines of code:

```
public function getFunctions()
{
    return [
        new \Twig_SimpleFunction('jslater', [$this, 'jslater']),
        new \Twig_SimpleFunction('jsnow', [$this, 'jsnow'])
    ];
}
public function jsnow()
{
    //...

}
```

In here, we would like to use the power of Twig to render a template that outputs all the `<script>` tags. Whenever Twig initializes an extension, if it is declared with the right methods, Twig will inject itself in the extension.

```
{% for script in scripts %}
<script type="text/javascript" src="{{script}}" />
{% endfor %}

class KhepinExtension extends \Twig_Extension
{
    protected $javascripts = [];

    public function initRuntime(\Twig_Environment $environment)
    {
        $this->environment = $environment;
    }

    public function getFunctions()
    {
        return [
```

```
                new \Twig_SimpleFunction('jslater', [$this, 'jslater']),
                new \Twig_SimpleFunction('jsnow', [$this, 'jsnow'])
            ];
    }

    public function jslater($src)
    {
        $this->javascripts[] = $src;
    }

    public function jsnow()
    {
        $template = 'KhepinBookBundle:Twig:javascripts.html.twig';
        return $this->environment->render($template, ['scripts' =>
$this->javascripts]);
    }

    public function getName()
    {
        return 'khepin_extension';
    }

}
```

The second part of our extension is now used as follows:

```
{{ jsnow() | raw }}
```

Testing a Twig extension

The format for testing a Twig extension is quite specific; you declare a test case that loads all your extensions and then define fixture files under a specific format.

```
use Khepin\BookBundle\Twig\KhepinExtension;
use Twig_Test_IntegrationTestCase;

class KhepinExtensionTest extends Twig_Test_IntegrationTestCase
{
    public function getExtensions()
    {
        return array(
            new KhepinExtension()
        );
    }

    public function getFixturesDir()
    {
```

```
        return __DIR__.'/Fixtures/';
    }

}
```

The fixtures then look as follows:

```
--TEST--
"jslater / jsnow" filter
--TEMPLATE--
{{jslater(script)}}
{{jslater(script)}}{{jsnow()|raw}}
--DATA--
return ['script' => 'jquery.js'];
--EXPECT--

<script type="text/javascript" src="jquery.js" />
```

This file defines the following:

- The test title
- A series of templates to be rendered
- The data to be passed to each template
- The expected results

However, running it will give us an error. Symfony, by default, loads templates from the filesystem based on a given convention—the `Bundle:Controller:template` format. This is fine, but during the tests, Twig doesn't know how to load this format. We'll refactor our class so that it can load the template directly as a string.

```
public function __construct()
{
    $this->environment = new \Twig_Environment(new \Twig_Loader_
String());
}

public function jsnow()
{
    $template = '{% for script in scripts %}<script type="text/
javascript" src="{{script}}" />{% endfor %}';

    $scripts = array_unique($this->javascripts);
    return $this->environment->render($template, compact('scripts'));

}
```

As we now create our own Twig environment to load templates as strings, we no longer need to call `initRuntime` and can use our own constructor.

The time difference filter

As an exercise, try to define a Twig extension for the following case:

On the home page, we want to display the activity of the website by showing who recently joined a meetup. Instead of showing "Molly joined Yoga Teachers Training on Nov 29 at 16:15", we'd like to show "Molly joined Yoga Teachers Training 5 minutes ago".

What we are trying to do is take an existing date, compare it to the current date, and format the output accordingly. Therefore, a filter seems to be the perfect extension type we need. Therefore, this time, we will be using the `\Twig_SimpleFilter` class.

Summary

With commands, we can now easily create tools for the developers who work on our application. We know that commands have access to the whole service container. We also know how to make them rely as much as possible on services, making the code for the command available to the whole application, if we need it later.

We only saw one form of extensions for templates but know that all other extension types (with the exception of custom tags) are just as easy and straightforward to implement. Custom tags are quite complex, and they are also very rarely needed. You can learn the basics of creating a new tag at `http://twig.sensiolabs.org/doc/advanced.html#tags`.

3
Forms

Symfony ships with a powerful form component. Building forms based on your classes, keeping the data in sync between a form and an object or any data structure, is a complicated topic. There are a few abstractions to understand how the form component works in order to enable its full power and make complete use of it.

One of the good things about it is that almost everything, once defined, is easily reusable. In the previous chapters, we were building a website that allows users to publish or join meetups. We stated at the outset that we wanted to show users only those meetups that are happening with a certain distance from them. For this, we had to know the actual location of each meetup and user. For users, we relied on their IP address, but for meetups, we should probably let the organizer define the exact address—maybe even on a map. There is no `map` input predefined in the form framework, so we will define one. It should be easy enough to reuse the same input in the user profile to know exactly where our user lives rather than relying on their IP.

An input for geographical coordinates

Our special field will use Google Maps and this will be the only part visible to the user. To achieve all this, since this is a rather complex widget, we will need all of the following four elements:

- A `Coordinate` class to hold our information
- A form type
- A Twig template
- A data transformer

In most cases, you will not need all of these. You have probably already defined form types without any of the other elements.

The Google Maps integration will be done by an external bundle available at `https://github.com/egeloen/IvoryGoogleMapBundle`.

The `Coordinate` class is quite straightforward and will not change much, so let's have a quick look at it in the following code:

```php
namespace Khepin\BookBundle\Geo;

use Ivory\GoogleMapBundle\Entity\Coordinate as GMapsCoordinate;

class Coordinate
{
    private $latitude;

    private $longitude;

    public function __construct($latitude = null, $longitude =
      null)
    {
        $this->latitude = $latitude;
        $this->longitude = $longitude;
    }

    public function getLatitude()
    {
        return $this->latitude;
    }

    public function setLatitude($latitude)
    {
        $this->latitude = $latitude;
    }

    public function getLongitude()
    {
        return $this->longitude;
    }

    public function setLongitude($longitude)
    {
        $this->longitude = $longitude;
    }
```

The default representation as a string should be `latitude, longitude`, as shown in the following code:

```
public function __toString()
{
    return '('.$this->latitude.', '.$this->longitude.')';
```

Based on the string representation (`latitude, longitude`), we will want to be able to create a new `Coordinate` instance using the following code:

```
public static function createFromString($string)
{
    if(strlen($string) < 1){
        return new self;
    }
    $string = str_replace(['(', ')', ' '], '', $string);
    $data = explode(',', $string);
    if($data[0] === "" || $data[1] === ""){
        return new self;
    }
    return new self($data[0], $data[1]);
}
```

We will need to convert this coordinate to the Google Maps version from the bundle using the following code. The reason we are not using it directly is that with our own `Coordinate` class, we can control and decide how to map it to a database later.

```
public function toGmaps()
{
    return new GMapsCoordinate($this->latitude, $this->longitude);
}
}
```

Setting up the basics

If you have ever built a form type, based on one of your entities for example, it probably looked like the one in the following code:

```
class CoordinateType extends AbstractType
{
    public function buildForm(FormBuilderInterface $builder, array
      $options)
    {
        // Build the form, add fields etc
    }
```

```
public function getName()
{
    return 'coordinate';
}

public function setDefaultOptions(OptionsResolverInterface
  $resolver)
{
  $resolver->setDefaults(['widget' => 'coordinate', 'compound'
    => false, 'data_class' =>
      'Khepin\BookBundle\Geo\Coordinate']);
}
}
```

We will keep the form like this for now and refer to this again whenever we need it. We have just done two simple things:

- We gave our form a name.
- We stated that the form should render using a special widget, `coordinate`. By default, you already have access to a certain number of widgets in Symfony. They are text fields, select boxes, checkboxes, and so on.

  We must set the `compound` option as it is true by default. The `compound` option should only be set to `true` when our field represents a collection that could contain any number of elements.

Our widget will display a map, and it already includes a hidden field. For now, we will define it in a very simple way at `Bundle/Resources/views/Form/widgets.html.twig`. Alternately, later on if you want to see what's happening in the hidden field, use `form_widget_simple` instead of `hidden_widget` in the template to replace the hidden field with a standard text field, as shown in the following code:

```
{% block coordinate_widget %}
    <div>Display the map here</div>
    {{ block('hidden_widget') }}
{% endblock %}
```

For Symfony (and Twig) to know about this widget, it needs to be added in the configuration under the `twig` section:

```
# Twig Configuration
twig:
    debug:            %kernel.debug%
    strict_variables: %kernel.debug%
    form:
        resources:
            - 'KhepinBookBundle:Form:widgets.html.twig'
```

Now that we have defined a coordinate type and its widget, we would like to try it. For trying this, we will have a simple controller and template in which we will use it as follows:

```
// Controller
public function mapAction()
{
    $form = $this->createFormBuilder()
        ->add('location', 'coordinate')
        ->add('submit', 'submit')
        ->getForm();
    $form = $form->createView();

    return compact('form');
}

{# Template #}
{% extends "::base.html.twig"%}

{% block body %}
    {{form(form)}}
{% endblock %}
```

If we were to try that though, we would get an exception informing us that the coordinate type is not defined. Indeed, we defined the class, but we tried to use it by referencing its name. What you normally do when you create a type class for your entities is that you define $this->createForm(new TaskType(),$task);, and you are in charge of instantiating the Type class yourself. For the types that are built in Symfony, you can just use their name. We aim to completely integrate our type into the framework, so this is what we want.

We need to tell the form framework that we have a special class somewhere that should be recognized as a form type. This is done in the exact same way as we previously told Twig that we had a special class that needed to be loaded as an extension through services and tags. Let's define a service for our form type and tag it properly using the following code:

```
khepin.form.type.coordinate:
    class: Khepin\BookBundle\Form\CoordinateType
    scope: prototype
    tags:
        - { name: form.type, alias: coordinate }
```

This is the first time we encounter the `prototype` scope. If you remember *Chapter 1, Services and Listeners*, we saw that the default scope is `container`, which always returns to you the same instance of a given class. But here, if we want to use that coordinate field more than once in a form (or per request), we need a new instance each time.

Now, loading our page will show our widget, although it doesn't do much yet.

Using the map

Our `type` class should prepare a `map` object and pass it on to the template. The template then has all the required logic to display it. In our controller, we see that to get the form in a way that can be used by the template, we call `getForm()` and then `createView()`. So, we need to get into that view creation process and add our map there. The map bundle we are using defines a service named `ivory_google_map.map` for creating maps from PHP. We inject this in our `Type` class and start adding the map to the view using the following code:

```
khepin.form.type.coordinate:
    class: Khepin\BookBundle\Form\CoordinateType
    scope: prototype
    arguments: [@ivory_google_map.map]
    tags:
        - { name: form.type, alias: coordinate }

class CoordinateType extends AbstractType
{
    protected $map;

    public function __construct($map)
    {
        $this->map = $map;
    }

    // Other methods unchanged omitted here

    public function buildView(FormView $view, FormInterface $form,
      array $options)
    {
        $center = new GMapsCoordinate(39.91311850372953,
          116.4002054820312);
        $this->map->setCenter($center);
        $this->map->setMapOption('zoom', 10);
```

```
            $view->vars['map'] = $this->map;
    }
}
```

We create the map and set the center to some sensible coordinates. We can also use the `user_locator` service we previously defined to set it to where the user is connecting from, or their exact address if we acquire it later. Also, when we are using this form to update an existing value, we will center the map on the existing coordinate. For now, we will change our widget as shown in the following code:

```
{% block coordinate_widget %}
    {{ google_map_container(map) }}
    {{ google_map_js(map) }}
    {% set read_only = true %}
    {{ block('form_widget_simple') }}
{% endblock %}
```

Now when we display the form, we can see our map!

We need a little bit of JavaScript so that our field will update every time we click on a point on the map. So, in the end, our widget could look as follows:

```
{% block coordinate_widget %}
    {{ google_map_container(map) }}
    {{ google_map_js(map) }}
    <script type="text/javascript">
        google.maps.event.addListener(
            {{map.javascriptVariable}}, {# The {{}} here is from
                Twig #}
            'click',
            setValue
        );
        function setValue(event) {
            var input = document.getElementById('{{id}}'); {# The
                {{}} here is from Twig #}
            input.value = event.latLng;
        }
    </script>
    {% set read_only = true %}
    {{ block('form_widget_simple') }}
{% endblock %}
```

Now, let's use our form and see what we get. We will display a map and the values from the last form submission, if any, using the following code:

```php
/**
 * @Route("/map")
 * @Template()
 */
public function mapAction(Request $request)
{
    $form = $this->createFormBuilder()
        ->add('location', 'coordinate')
        ->getForm();
    $location = null;

    if ($request->getMethod() === 'POST') {
        $form->handleRequest($request);
        $location = $form->getData()['location'];
    }
    $form = $form->createView();
    return compact('form', 'location');
}
```

```twig
{% extends "::base.html.twig"%}

{% block body %}
Latitude: {{location.latitude}} - Longitude: {{location.longitude}}

{{form_start(form)}}
    {{form_row(form.location)}}
    {{form_rest(form)}}
    <button type="submit">Submit</button>
{{form_end(form)}}
{% endblock %}
```

So far, it all works, except that the data we retrieve for the location is a string, and we would like to actually have it as a `Coordinate` object instead.

Data transformers

By using data transformers, the form components in Symfony offer a powerful way of dealing with this scenario. The form component allows three distinct representations of the same data, which are as follows:

- The one in the view (in the HTML)
- The one in the model
- The one in the form itself (if necessary)

In most cases, this is overkill. For our current case, only one transformer will be enough to go from a string (such as 42.0321650 and 115.032160513) to the PHP object representation. However, if you think about date and time, it can be that your form offers the choice that the view shows three select boxes for the year, month, and day; a datepicker; or a timestamp-based value. At the same time, you can expect that your PHP model object always needs it as a string based on a certain format. If you want to create a form type that offers this kind of flexibility, it's better if the form internally keeps everything as a DateTime object, and then transforms it for the view or the model.

Data transformers have only two methods: transform and reverseTransform. The transform method goes from the model to the form and from the form to the view. The reverseTransform method goes from the view to the form and from the form to the model. The following diagram represents the flow of two methods:

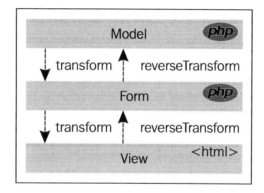

Consider the following code snippet:

```php
namespace Khepin\BookBundle\Form\Transformer;

use Symfony\Component\Form\DataTransformerInterface;
use Symfony\Component\Form\Exception\TransformationFailedException;
use Khepin\BookBundle\Geo\Coordinate;

class GeoTransformer implements DataTransformerInterface
{
    public function transform($geo)
    {
        return $geo;
    }

    public function reverseTransform($latlong)
```

```
        {
            return Coordinate::createFromString($latlong);
        }
    }
```

The `transform` method will not do anything as our class already implements a `toString()` method that will directly render the view value. The `reverseTransform` method does the opposite by creating a `Coordinate` object from a string.

Now, we will add our transformer to the coordinate form type, update the view, and build the map using the data from the form instead of a predefined location so that while editing the form, the map will be centered on the previously chosen coordinates:

```
public function buildForm(FormBuilderInterface $builder, array
  $options)
{
    $builder->addViewTransformer(new GeoTransformer);
}

public function buildView(FormView $view, FormInterface $form, array
  $options)
{
    $center = new GMapsCoordinate($form->getData()->getLatitude(),
      $form->getData()->getLongitude());
    $this->map->setCenter($center);
    $this->map->setMapOption('zoom', 10);

    $view->vars['map'] = $this->map;
}
```

Since `Coordinate` implements a `__toString()` method, there will be no difference on the template. However, if you try to dump the object that we get from the form, you can see that it is actually a `Coordinate` object.

One last thing we would like to improve is that currently we have set the default location to something predefined. However, in *Chapter 1, Services and Listeners,* we created a service that helps us determine where a user is located based on their IP address. It would be nicer to use this and set the default map location to the one the user is likely connecting from instead of setting it to a predefined value.

Forms based on user data

We had previously defined our form type as a service, so now we will change its configuration for it to take the `user_locator` service as the second argument, as shown in the following code:

```
khepin.form.type.coordinate:
    class: Khepin\BookBundle\Form\CoordinateType
    scope: prototype
    arguments: [@ivory_google_map.map, @user_locator]
    tags:
        - { name: form.type, alias: coordinate }
```

If you recall correctly, the `user_locator` service was in the `request` scope, but our form type is in the `prototype` scope. Since the `prototype` scope is more restrictive than the `request` scope, we don't have any issues here.

We will also update the default values of `CoordinateType` using the following code so that it always has a default value, which will be an empty coordinate:

```
public function setDefaultOptions(OptionsResolverInterface $resolver)
{
    $resolver->setDefaults([
        'widget' => 'coordinate',
        'compound' => false,
        'data_class' => 'Khepin\BookBundle\Geo\Coordinate',
        'data' => new Coordinate(),
    ]);
}
```

There are many places where we can change that default value to a new value before displaying the form. We can change the way in which we build `GMapsCoordinate` in the `buildView` function. This will work technically, but it will be better to have the form to display its value normally.

The form framework in Symfony uses events. They're not sent through the Symfony kernel though, and are specific to each form. Each class or function that wants to listen to an event on the form has to be declared in that form or form type. We can declare them as event subscribers or as anonymous functions, which we will be using here.

There are five possible events described as follows:

- PRE_SET_DATA: This event is triggered before the data is bound to the form and allows you to change the data. If you are editing an object, it is likely that there will be some data to be set. When you are using a blank form, the data will usually be empty or will only contain default values.

- POST_SET_DATA: This event allows you to perform some actions after the data has been set in the form.

- PRE_SUBMIT: This event lets you modify the form before submission.

- SUBMIT: This event allows you to perform some actions on form submission.

- POST_SUBMIT: This event lets you perform actions after the form has been submitted.

In our case, of course, we can only use PRE_SET_DATA since anything after that would be too late! The following code shows exactly how to do this in the Form class:

```php
public function buildForm(FormBuilderInterface $builder, array
    $options)
{
    $builder->addModelTransformer(new GeoTransformer);

    $builder->addEventListener(FormEvents::PRE_SET_DATA,
        function(FormEvent $event) use ($builder) {
            $data = $event->getData();

            if (null === $data->getLatitude()) {
                $geocoded = $this->locator->getUserCoordinates();
                $value = new Coordinate($geocoded->getLatitude();
                $geocoded->getLongitude());
                $event->setData($value);
            }
    });
}
```

 The getUserCoordinates method of the user_locator service was not implemented in *Chapter 1, Services and Listeners*. The implementation shouldn't be a problem for you at this point of the book.

If the data has latitude that is not null, it is not coming from our default value, so we don't need to modify it in any way. If it is empty, however, we replace it with the coordinates of the current user.

Going further

For the last part of this chapter, we will go a bit further with the customization of forms.

A part of our meetups website requires a user to enter their house address so that they can receive a membership card that will be directly sent out to them. Since we already have a relatively good idea where that user is coming from, we will preset the country for them in the form. Here, we only differentiate between users coming from within or outside the USA to decide if they must fill in the state they are coming from.

The initial setup

Our `Address` class is very simple and contains only a few attributes as well as getters and setters, as shown in the following code snippet:

```
class Address
{
    protected $id;

    protected $street;

    protected $number;

    protected $country;

    protected $state;

    protected $zip;

    // public function getXxx();
    // public function setXxx($x);
}
```

The basic form class will be as shown in the following code:

```
class AddressType extends AbstractType
{
    public function buildForm(FormBuilderInterface $builder, array
     $options)
    {
        $state_options = [
            'AL' => 'Alabama',
```

```
        // ...
        'WY' => 'Wyoming'
    ];
    $builder
        ->add('street')
        ->add('number')
        ->add('country', 'choice', [
            'choices' => [
                'US' => 'USA',
                'OTHER' => 'Not USA'
            ]
        ])
        ->add('state', 'choice', [
            'choices' => $state_options
        ])
        ->add('zip')
    ;
}

public function setDefaultOptions(OptionsResolverInterface
 $resolver)
{
    $resolver->setDefaults(array(
        'data_class' => 'Khepin\BookBundle\Entity\Address'
    ));
}

public function getName()
{
    return 'address';
}
}
```

In the controller, we only set a default value for the country while displaying an empty form. If it is a POST request, the user will have picked a country when using the form; therefore, we can avoid this step and a long network call to a GeoIP provider. We have, of course, created a controller to display this form, as shown in the following code:

```
/**
 * @Route("/address")
 * @Template()
 */
public function addressAction(Request $request)
{
```

```
$message = '';
$form = null;

$address = new \Khepin\BookBundle\Entity\Address;

if ($request->getMethod() === 'GET') {
    $country = $this->get('user_locator')
      ->getCountryCode();
    $address->setCountry($country);
}

$form = $this->createForm(new AddressType, $address, [
  'action' => '',
  'method' => 'POST',
]);

if ($request->getMethod() === 'POST') {
    $form->handleRequest($request);
    if ($form->isValid()) {
        $message = 'The form is valid';
    }
}

$form = $form->createView();
return compact('form', 'message');
}
```

We have also included a message in the template to know if the form is valid or not. This will be important very soon. So far, everything should look pretty straightforward to anyone having worked with Symfony.

Adding and removing fields

We will now customize the form based on its own data. If we already know that the country is the USA, we add a field for the state; otherwise, we don't.

 In a more realistic scenario, you would probably want to always have the field and decide in the frontend if you want to show it or not, as this would allow the user to directly decide this.

Modifying a form based on its current data is actually a very common scenario. The most common use is to allow different actions when a record is created from when it is only edited. If the user already has an ID, we add or remove certain fields. Every form where you pass in a hidden field with the ID of another object, such as a form to subscribe to a specific event or a form to message a given friend, can be a good case for this.

We will update our form, as follows, to have the state field added or not depending on the country:

```php
public function buildForm(FormBuilderInterface $builder, array
  $options)
{
    $state_options = [
            'choices' => [
                'AL' => 'Alabama',
                // ...
                'WY' => 'Wyoming',
            ]
    ];

    $builder
        ->add('street')
        ->add('number')
        ->add('country', 'choice', [
            'choices' => [
                'US' => 'USA',
                'OTHER' => 'Not USA'
            ]
        ])
        ->add('zip')
    ;

    $builder->addEventListener(FormEvents::PRE_SET_DATA,
      function(FormEvent $event) use ($state_options){
        $address = $event->getData();
        if ($address === null) {
            return;
        }

        if ($address->getCountry() == 'US') {
            $event->getForm()->add('state', 'choice',
            $state_options);
        }
    });
}
```

This seems to be good; however, if you were to actually try it with an IP address coming from the USA, you will realize that after submitting the form, it is not valid. Let's dig a bit into what happens during the first request (showing the empty form) and the second one (sending data to the form):

Display	Submit
Creates an address with country as the USA.	Creates an address with no specified country.
Builds the form.	Builds the form.
On PRE_SET_DATA, we have an address with country as the US, so we add a field to pick a state.	On PRE_SET_DATA, we have an empty address. This is the data that we passed while instantiating the form. The data submitted by the user is sent on BIND. We don't add the state field.
Done	The form is bound to the submitted data.
Done	The form is validated, but the submitted data has one additional field named state, so it is invalid.

Whenever we modify a form based on its own values, we must make sure to modify it at two points in time:

- Before we set the initial data in the form
- Before we bind the form to actual user-submitted data

This way, we can ensure that the user's data will be validated against the right representation of our form.

We'll add a second listener to our form, as shown in the following code snippet, so that if the data submitted by the user has the USA as a country, we will also allow the list of states on the form:

```
$builder->addEventListener(FormEvents::PRE_SUBMIT, function(FormEvent
$event) use ($state_options){
    $address = $event->getData();

    if ($address['country'] == 'US') {
        $event->getForm()->add('state', 'choice', $state_options);
    }
});
```

The event data is an array and not an object. It will be available as an object only after the form has been bound. However, after that, we cannot modify the structure of the form anymore and wouldn't be able to add the `state` field.

Now, our form can be displayed and submitted as we expect!

Summary

This chapter presented an in-depth view of the possibilities offered to you by the form framework within Symfony. It might seem a complex thing at first, but if you understand the basic parts, it's easy to find your way around.

You can now create your own form widgets that can be used just as any of the base widgets, treating a map as a new type of input field. You also know how to use a data transformer in order to have different representations of the same information that fit within the model, the form, or the view. If you want to practice your form skills, you can try some of the following:

- Create a form for messaging that includes an AJAX field for friend selection
- Create a form that accepts a collection of our coordinate type

Now that we have a good hold on many extension possibilities in Symfony, it is time to get into one of the most technical and difficult topics: **Security**. There is a lot to be said since security can be understood in many ways and touches many areas of your application, from the forms to how you store records in your database.

4
Security

Security is a very broad topic, and in general, it means restricting access to resources depending on who tries to access them. This chapter will not be going into the theory but will be a hands-on approach on how you can customize the security layer of Symfony to meet your needs.

Security is usually split into two parts:

- **Authentication**: This identifies who is trying to access our app and is a prerequisite to authorization
- **Authorization**: It decides if a user has the right to access specific parts of the app/data

In other words, authentication answers the question "Who are you?" (Luke SkyWalker) and authorization decides what you are allowed to do (for example, Use the force: yes; Pilot the Death Star: no).

We'll first go through both the topics in order, and then see a practical application of these techniques to protect an API against CSRF attacks.

Authentication

There are many ways to authenticate a user. The most common pattern nowadays is through the username and password, but we also have the third-party sites' authentication (Facebook login, Twitter login, GitHub, and so on), which sometimes uses OAuth or their custom method. LDAP is also a popular option in the enterprise.

Symfony's documentation already contains everything you need to know about creating a custom authentication. However, it is hard to understand why you are doing things in a particular way when following the official guide. This part guides you through the same process, while detailing the reasons why things are done in such a way, and how each part connects with each other.

Simple OAuth with GitHub

In this part, we'll add authentication through GitHub's API; GitHub implements OAuth. How this works in practice is that your app will contain a link to send users to a GitHub page asking them if they want to allow your app to connect to their GitHub account (only if they haven't yet) and then redirect them to a given URL. From this URL, we need to retrieve information about the user and log them in. We'll make a simple controller do this first and ensure things are working correctly. As we need to communicate to the GitHub servers over HTTP, we included the Guzzle library (http://guzzle.readthedocs.org/en/latest/) that helps deal with HTTP communication.

 If you are unfamiliar with OAuth, you might want to learn about the basics (http://en.wikipedia.org/wiki/OAuth) before diving into this chapter so that you get a better understanding of how the process is happening.

Before you start, you need to create an app on GitHub, which will give you a client_id and a secret_token. Then, we will create our simple controller as follows:

```
/**
 * @Route("/github")
 */
public function ghloginAction(Request $request)
{
    $client = new \Guzzle\Http\Client(
        'https://github.com/login/oauth/access_token');
    $req = $client->post('', null, [
        'client_id' => 'your app client_id',
        'client_secret' => 'your app secret_token',
        'code' => $request->query->get('code')
    ])->setHeader('Accept', 'application/json');

    $res = $req->send()->json();
    $token = $res['access_token'];

    $client = new \Guzzle\Http\Client(
        'https://api.github.com');
    $req = $client->get('/user');
    $req->getQuery()->set('access_token', $token);
    $username = $req->send()->json()['login'];

    return new Response($username);
}
```

Then, if you point the URL to `https://github.com/login/oauth/ authorize?client_id=<client_id>&redirect_uri=http://your-project. local/github`, you will be on GitHub and will be asked if you want to allow this application (your project) to use your GitHub account. After you allow it, you are redirected to `http://your-project.local/github`.

 You only allow the app once. After that, GitHub will automatically redirect you to the right page.

When GitHub redirects you, it adds a code query string to the URL so that it actually looks like `http://your-project.local/github?code=<some code>`.

With that code, we ask GitHub for an `access_token` token specific to this user. This token now allows us to browse GitHub's API as if we were that user. We request the special URL `https://api.github.com/user`, which returns the current user information (username, ID, and so on).

If everything worked correctly, you will see your GitHub username on the screen. Great! Now, we need to hook this process inside Symfony's security layer. Now that we understood the basic principle inside, let's make it work with the actual Symfony authentication mechanisms, starting with Symfony's firewall.

The firewall

Firewalls in Symfony are configured so that they know which parts of the application are free to visit and which require a user to be authenticated (defined by a URL pattern). The firewall only cares about authentication. Whenever a request arrives to a URL, the firewall checks if this URL can be visited by anonymous users (in which case, the request flows through). If the URL requires authenticated users, the request either flows through (the user is already authenticated), or the firewall interrupts it and initiates the authentication process.

To authenticate users, you declare a special URL in Symfony's firewall. This URL does not map to a controller. The firewall catches it, finds which class is listening for it, and asks it to authenticate the user. Our firewall configuration now looks like the following code snippet:

```
firewalls:
    main:
        pattern: ^/.*
        form_login:
            provider: fos_userbundle
            csrf_provider: form.csrf_provider
        github:
```

```
                check_path: /github_login
        logout:        true
        anonymous:     true
```

The `/github_login` part, although not mapped to a controller, is quite important here. We will use it as the `redirect_url` parameter when we go to log in from GitHub. If you start to have multiple OAuth providers, you can then clearly separate them to implement a login for each of them.

At the same time, we need to declare this route in `routing.yml`, but again, it does not need to be tied to a controller:

```
# routing.yml
github_login:
    pattern: /github_login
```

Next, we need to create an authentication listener that will listen on this special URL and tell Symfony about it. Symfony provides an abstract class for `AuthenticationListener`, which means we won't have to implement all the methods. All we have to do is implement the `attemptAuthentication` method. For this, we'll reuse the code that is placed in the controller:

```php
namespace Khepin\BookBundle\Security\Github;

use Symfony\Component\Security\Http\Firewall\
AbstractAuthenticationListener;
use Khepin\BookBundle\Security\Github\GithubUserToken;
use Symfony\Component\HttpFoundation\Request;

class AuthenticationListener extends AbstractAuthenticationListener
{
    protected function attemptAuthentication(Request $request)
    {
        $client = new \Guzzle\Http\Client(
            'https://github.com/login/oauth/access_token');
        $req = $client->post('', null, [
            'client_id' => 'xxx',
            'client_secret' => 'xxx',
            'code' => $request->query->get('code')
        ])->setHeader('Accept', 'application/json');

        $res = $req->send()->json();
        $access_token = $res['access_token'];

        $client = new \Guzzle\Http\Client(
            'https://api.github.com');
```

```
$req = $client->get('/user');
$req->getQuery()
    ->set('access_token', $access_token);
$email = $req->send()->json()['email'];

$token = new GithubUserToken();
$token->setCredentials($email)

return $this->authenticationManager
            ->authenticate($token);
    }
}
```

One more class again! The code is exactly what we had before, except that this time, instead of returning the response, we return a token. The token now only holds the user's credentials. In this case, we have retrieved the user's e-mail address and set it in the token.

By using GitHub or any other third party, we no longer need a password. We trust that when GitHub says **user@example.com is trying to connect**, it has already verified this. We can then create a simplified Token class that only contains the e-mail and no password.

The token itself is fairly simple:

```
namespace Khepin\BookBundle\Security\Github;
use Symfony\Component\Security\Core\Authentication\Token\
AbstractToken;

class GithubUserToken extends AbstractToken
{
    private $credentials;

    public function setCredentials($email)
    {
        $this->credentials = $email;
    }

    public function getCredentials()
    {
        return $this->credentials;
    }
}
```

We use the user's e-mail because if we find the same user e-mail from GitHub and Twitter logins, we know it is actually the same user. But finding the same username doesn't mean much; it could be two different people who registered the same name for different services.

The security factory

We already wrote two new classes and a bit of configuration, and yet, if you try to load your application right now, all you will see is an error stating that "GitHub" is not a recognized option for the firewall. So we need to keep working on this for a bit longer before we can see anything. That's why we tried things within a controller first so that we can immediately see what worked and what didn't.

So far, we have defined the following options:

- The token
- The authentication listener

Now, we need to tell the firewall how to make any use of these. The class responsible for tying these together is `SecurityFactory`.

Let's take a look at how things work for the security component. In the following diagram, we can see that **Factory** brings together the `AuthenticationListener` and `UserProvider` classes and makes the firewall aware of them:

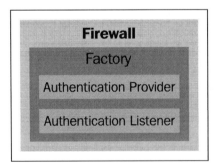

In the following diagram, we see that any incoming request is first stopped at the **Firewall** level. The firewall finds a suitable authentication listener for this request, which creates a non-authenticated token with all the relevant information in order to authenticate the user later. This token is then passed on to the **User Provider** block, which attempts to find a user based on the given credentials.

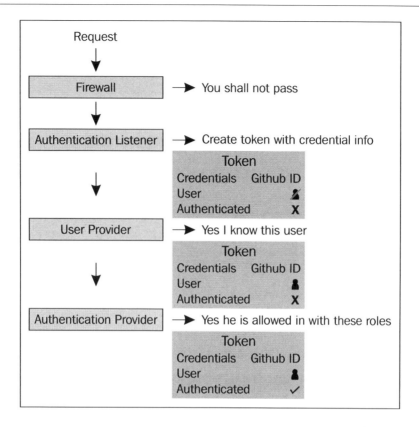

To define our security factory, we extend it from the abstract security factory, thus avoiding the burden of reimplementing everything. This is shown in the following code:

```
namespace Khepin\BookBundle\Security\Github\SecurityFactory;

use Symfony\Bundle\SecurityBundle\DependencyInjection\
    Security\Factory\AbstractFactory;
use Symfony\Component\DependencyInjection\ContainerBuilder;
use Symfony\Component\DependencyInjection\DefinitionDecorator;
use Symfony\Component\DependencyInjection\Reference;

class SecuirtyFactory extends AbstractFactory
{
    public function createAuthProvider(
        ContainerBuilder $container, $id, $config,
            $userProviderId)
    {
```

```
            $providerId =
                'khepin.github.authentication_provider.'.$id;
            $definition = $container->setDefinition(
                $providerId, new DefinitionDecorator(
                    'khepin.github.authentication_provider')
            );
            if (isset($config['provider']))
            {
                $definition->addArgument(new Reference(
                    $userProviderId));
            }

            return $providerId;
        }

        public function getPosition()
        {
            return 'pre_auth';
        }

        public function getKey()
        {
            return 'github';
        }

        protected function getListenerId()
        {
            return 'khepin.github.authentication_listener';
        }
    }
```

The getKey method returns the name under which you will be able to use the security factory in the firewall. The createAuthProvider part receives the builder for the dependency injection container and can add and modify service definitions. Here, a new authentication provider is created, and we pass the user_provider parameter as an argument to its constructor.

The preceding class is then passed onto your Bundle class, the one that Symfony generates at the root of each bundle, to be added to the configuration, which is shown in the following code snippet. We will see more about what it means to add configuration directly through the Bundle class in *Chapter 6, Sharing Your Extensions*.

```
namespace Khepin\BookBundle;

use Symfony\Component\HttpKernel\Bundle\Bundle;
use Khepin\BookBundle\Security\Github\SecurityFactory;
```

```
class KhepinBookBundle extends Bundle
{
    public function build(ContainerBuilder $container)
    {
        parent::build($container);

        $extension = $container->getExtension('security');
        $extension->addSecurityListenerFactory(
    new SecurityFactory()
        );
    }
}
```

This part, at least, is pretty straightforward to understand.

There is one last class that must be implemented before we can finish our configuration and use our login, the AuthenticationProvider class, which is given in the following code snippet:

```
namespace Khepin\BookBundle\Security\Github;

use Symfony\Component\Security\Core\Authentication
    \Provider\AuthenticationProviderInterface;
use Symfony\Component\Security\Core\Authentication
    \Token\TokenInterface;
use Khepin\BookBundle\Security\Github\GithubUserToken;

class AuthenticationProvider implements
    AuthenticationProviderInterface
{
    private $user_provider;

    public function __construct($user_provider)
    {
        $this->user_provider = $user_provider;
    }

    public function supports(TokenInterface $token)
    {
        return $token instanceof GithubUserToken;
    }

    public function authenticate(TokenInterface $token)
    {
```

```
        $email = $token->getCredentials();
        $user = $this->user_provider->loadOrCreate($username);
        // Log the user in
        $new_token = new GithubUserToken($user->getRoles());
        $new_token->setUser($user);
        $new_token->setAuthenticated(true);
        return $new_token;
    }
}
```

It receives a user provider that is used to either load or create the user. This is because a login through GitHub or any third-party site can be as much a login as it can be a registration. So, if the user is not found, it must be created. Letting Symfony know that the user is now authenticated means two things on the token, which are as follows:

- The `Token::isAuthenticated` line is `true`

- The token contains some roles defining what the user is or isn't allowed to do within the application

The services configuration is as follows:

```
khepin.github.authentication_listener:
    class: Khepin\BookBundle\Security\Github\
        AuthenticationListener
    parent: security.authentication.listener.abstract
    abstract: true
    public: false

khepin.github.authentication_provider:
    class: Khepin\BookBundle\Security\Github\
        AuthenticationProvider
    public: false
```

There are two interesting aspects we didn't see before. They are as follows:

- `parent`: This service definition inherits from another service definition, so anything that is not specified directly here will come from the parent.

- `abstract`: This service itself cannot be implemented. The security component is responsible for taking this abstract service definition and creating actual concrete services from it.

Our security file now also looks like the following code snippet:

```
providers:
    fos_userbundle:
```

```
            id: fos_user.user_provider.username

firewalls:
    main:
        pattern: ^/
        form_login:
            provider: fos_userbundle
            csrf_provider: form.csrf_provider
        github:
            provider: fos_userbundle
            check_path: /github_login
        logout:         true
        anonymous:      true
```

As FOSUserBundle is a very popular way of dealing with users in Symfony, we are reusing their user provider. This would work fine if your users were already registered with the same username they have on GitHub and if we were using the username to identify users. However, we need to use the e-mails to ensure consistent and secure logins through multiple third-party providers.

> The UserProvider class is one of the components of Symfony's security component, so you don't need the one provided by FOSUserBundle. It is used in this example for convenience and shows how you can integrate your new authentication with it.

We can then create our own user provider using the following code snippet:

```php
class UserProvider implements UserProviderInterface
{
    public function __construct($user_manager)
    {
        $this->user_manager = $user_manager;
    }

    public function supportsClass($class)
    {
        return $this->user_manager->supportsClass($class);
    }

    public function loadUserByUsername($email)
    {
        $user = $this->user_manager->findUserByEmail($email);
```

```
        if (empty ($user)) {
            $user = $this->user_manager->createUser();
            $user->setEnabled (true);
            $user->setPassword ('');
            $user->setEmail ($email);
            $user->setUsername ($email);
        }
        $this->user_manager->updateUser ($user);

        return $user;
    }

    public function loadOrCreateUser ($email)
    {
        return $this->loadUserByUsername ($email);
    }

    public function refreshUser (UserInterface $user)
    {
        if (!$this->supportsClass (get_class ($user)) ||
            !$user->getEmail ())
        {
            throw new UnsupportedUserException (sprintf (
            'Instances of "%s" are not supported.',
            get_class ($user)));
        }

        return $this->loadUserByUsername ($user->getEmail ());
    }
}
```

The preceding UserProvider class is then defined as a service and is set up as a provider in the security configuration. This is done using the following lines of code:

```
# config.yml
khepin.github.user_provider:
    class: Khepin\BookBundle\Security\Github\UserProvider
    arguments: [@fos_user.user_manager]

# security.yml
providers:
    fos_userbundle:
        id: fos_user.user_provider.username
    github_provider:
```

```
            id: khepin.github.user_provider

    firewalls:
        main:
            pattern: ^/
            form_login:
                provider: fos_userbundle
                csrf_provider: form.csrf_provider
            github:
                provider: github_provider
                check_path: /github_login
            logout:        true
            anonymous:     true
```

Authentication is not the easiest part to understand in Symfony, but it is structured in a way that allows for many customizations. After this part, you should have a better understanding of how things are working and be able to create your own authentication method if you need it.

Authorization

It is a common thing in any application to restrict access to different parts of an application depending on who the user is. In Symfony, this can be done in many places, such as through **annotations** on the controller (or some equivalent configuration), via **Access Control Lists (ACL)**, and through **voters**.

Controller annotations are role-based, which is fine for a lot of cases, but won't be adapted when we want to exercise fine-grained controls. At that point, you either have to create many more roles to express all of the permissions of a user or start using ACLs. ACLs provide much more fine-grained control, but they are very inexpressive. A user's rights on a given object or page are stored in the database as just that; these rights are called granular permissions. These permissions have to be granted and revoked one by one in your code; so, if you decide one day to completely change the logic of how some users are allowed to do something and others are not, you will have to go over all of these single permissions again and update them.

Voters in Symfony allow you to express your permissions as business logic rules. Some famous websites (think *stackoverflow*, for example) rely on this type of logic a lot. A user with a reputation of less than 100 cannot edit a question, a user with a reputation of 1000 or more can close a question, and so on. Luckily, in Symfony, it doesn't really matter how you express your authorization logic; the way to check a user's rights to perform an action or access a resource is always done in the same way through `SecurityContext`; for example, consider the following code lines:

```
$context->isGranted('ROLE_ADMIN');
$context->isGranted('EDIT', $object);
```

Our project so far was to create meetups that a user can join. As we're a small website for now, we don't plan to grow international operations yet. So, we'll only allow users from a given country to create new meetups. Anyone can create a meetup as long as they are from the right country.

 In real life, it is very difficult to know which country a user is actually from. The IP address checks can be circumvented by using VPN services, and everything else coming in the HTTP request to your server can be set up by anyone with basic knowledge of HTTP. You shouldn't base any important security decisions on that information.

Voters

Let's create a simple `Voter` class that will let a user create a meetup depending on their country. The `Voter` class implements the three methods of `VoterInterface`, which are as follows:

- `supportsAttribute`: This method will return true if the attribute is `MEETUP_CREATE`, and false otherwise. This means our voter is only allowed to vote for this. It will not be called when the security component is checking for something else such as `ROLE_ADMIN`, for example. It's important to set it correctly to avoid conflicts between different voters.

- `supportsClass`: This method will return `true` all the time as we won't be passed an actual object to check if the user has rights on this specific object.

- `vote`: This method will return the result of our vote.

 As you will see, it is your responsibility to call the `supports*` methods; the `AccessDecisionManager` method will not do it for you.

```php
namespace Khepin\BookBundle\Security\Voters;

use Symfony\Component\HttpFoundation\RequestStack;
use Symfony\Component\Security\Core\Authorization
        \Voter\VoterInterface;
use Symfony\Component\Security\Core\Authentication
        \Token\TokenInterface;

class CountryVoter implements VoterInterface
{
    protected $country_code;

    public function __construct($service_container)
    {
        $this->country_code = $service_container
      ->get('user_locator')->getCountryCode();
    }

    public function supportsAttribute($attribute)
    {
        return $attribute === 'MEETUP_CREATE';
    }

    public function supportsClass($class)
    {
        return true;
    }

    public function vote(TokenInterface $token, $object, array
$attributes)
    {
        if ( !$this->supportsClass(get_class($object)) ||
        !$this->supportsAttribute($attributes[0])
      ) {
            return VoterInterface::ACCESS_ABSTAIN;
        }
        if ($this->country_code === 'CN') {
            return VoterInterface::ACCESS_GRANTED;
        }
        return VoterInterface::ACCESS_DENIED;
    }
}
```

The vote method of a voter can return one of the following three results:

- ACCESS_GRANTED: The user is allowed access
- ACCESS_DENIED: The user is denied access
- ACCESS_ABSTAIN: This voter does not take part in the current vote

We define this voter as a service and tag it as a security voter using the following lines of code:

```
security.access.country_voter:
    class:       Khepin\BookBundle\Security\Voters\CountryVoter
    public:      false
    arguments:   [@service_container]
    tags:
        - { name: security.voter }
```

If you haven't done it before, it is now time to use the AccessDecisionManager method in the security configuration using the following code lines:

```
security:
    access_decision_manager:
        strategy:  unanimous
```

As shown in the preceding code lines, AccessDecisionManager takes a few possible arguments, which are described as follows:

- strategy: This can have one of the following values:
    - unanimous: If any voter votes ACCESS_DENIED, then access is denied
    - affirmative: If any voter votes ACCESS_GRANTED, then access is granted
    - consensus: This counts the number of ACCESS_DENIED and ACCESS_GRANTED permissions and decides based on the majority of votes
- allow_if_all_abstain: This checks whether or not to grant access when all voters returned ACCESS_ABSTAIN
- allow_if_equal_granted_denied: In the consensus strategy, when the number of ACCESS_GRANTED and ACCESS_DENIED is equal, this checks whether access should be granted or not

The last step to make this work is to configure the controller to deny access to anyone who isn't allowed to create a meetup:

```
/**
 * @Security("is_granted('MEETUP_CREATE')")
```

```
 * ... other annotations ...
 */
public function newAction()
{
    // ...
}
```

The logic we implemented here would be painful to manage through roles or ACL. With these, whenever you want to add a new country, you would have to find all users in that country and update their roles or ACL. You would also need to update all of the users' entries in the ACL whenever they change country and so forth.

Voters can also be used for more specific object decisions. If our meetups had to be reviewed and then published or approved by someone else, we would need specific permission checks for this. However, maybe a user that has already successfully organized at least five meetups can now be trusted to publish them on their own. These would work exactly the same way as what we just saw as they are rules independent from the meetup itself.

A different case would happen if we decide that a user can only update a meetup if the following conditions are met:

- They were the ones who created the meetup.
- The meetup has not been joined by anyone yet. This would avoid bad surprises for users who joined a meetup.

First, let's see how the `AccessDecisionManager` strategies work if we modify our edit controller to include the following code snippet:

```
if (!$this->get('security.context')
    ->isGranted('EDIT', $entity)) {
  throw new UnauthorizedHttpException(
    'No edit allowed at this time'
  );
}
```

Trying to access the edit page, we get an unauthorized response. This happened because all our voters abstained from voting and we didn't set `allow_if_all_abstain` to true. Try switching it to see the effect, then set it back to false before we continue.

Since the voter has already passed the security token while voting, we don't need to inject it while defining the service; hence, our service definition is extremely simple:

```
security.access.meetup_voter:
    class:      Khepin\BookBundle\Security\Voters\MeetupVoter
    public:     false
    tags:
        - { name: security.voter }
```

The voter class now becomes as follows:

```php
namespace Khepin\BookBundle\Security\Voters;

use Symfony\Component\HttpFoundation\RequestStack;
use Symfony\Component\Security\Core\Authorization\Voter\
    VoterInterface;
use Symfony\Component\Security\Core\Authentication\Token\
    TokenInterface;

class MeetupVoter implements VoterInterface
{
    public function supportsAttribute($attribute)
    {
        return $attribute === 'EDIT';
    }

    public function supportsClass($class)
    {
        return $class === 'Khepin\BookBundle\Entity\Event';
    }

    public function vote(TokenInterface $token, $object,
        array $attributes)
    {
        if (!$this->supportsClass(get_class($object)) ||
            !$this->supportsAttribute($attributes[0]))
        {
            return VoterInterface::ACCESS_ABSTAIN;
        }

        if (
            $this->meetupHasNoAttendees($object) &&
                $this->isMeetupCreator($token->getUser(), $object))
            {
                return VoterInterface::ACCESS_GRANTED;
            }
```

```
        return VoterInterface::ACCESS_DENIED;
    }

    protected function meetupHasNoAttendees($meetup)
    {
        return $meetup->getAttendees()->count() === 0;
    }

    protected function isMeetupCreator($user, $meetup)
    {
        return $user->getUserId() === $meetup->getUserId();
    }
}
```

Any user is now allowed to edit a meetup if and only if they are the organizer of that meetup and the meetup does not have any attendees yet. These complex decision rules would be impossible to express through roles. They could be expressed with ACLs and with a lot of care. They could be repeated over different controllers too. With voters, you have a simple way to use access rules that are very expressive and simple to use.

We saw that to secure our controller action, all we had to do was to add an @Security annotation. Annotations are a very common way of configuring things in Symfony, and we have already encountered them in the book (defining controllers in *Chapter 1, Services and Listeners*), but never written our own. The @Security annotation is also interesting because it does more than just provide some configuration information about a method or a class; it modifies the workflow of the application, adding a security check before the method is executed.

Annotations

Let's take advantage of this possibility in our app. An event organizer should be able to contact the event attendees and view their phone numbers in case of last minute changes to the event. Therefore, we should only allow users that have registered their phone number in their profile to join an event.

Our action to join an event should be decorated with an annotation as follows:

```
/**
 * @Route("/events/{event_id}/join")
 * @Template()
 * @ValidateUser("join_event")
 */
```

```
public function joinAction($event_id) {
    // ...
}
```

Here, `join_event` is the name of the validation group, which is defined in the user class as follows:

```
/**
 * @ORM\Column(type="string", length=255, name="phone")
 * @Assert\NotBlank(groups={"join_event"})
 */
protected $phone;
```

Defining an annotation

Annotations are defined through annotation classes. These classes don't need to inherit or implement any specific interface, but they need to be annotated with `@Annotation`.

An annotation will receive an array as a constructor parameter. This array contains all the information that was passed to the annotation. Consider that your annotation is as follows:

```
/**
 * @Log("custom_logger", level="debug")
 */
```

Then, the array you would receive in the constructor would be:

```
[ 'value' => 'custom_logger', 'level' => 'debug']
```

Whenever you need to read an annotation, you need an annotation reader. Of course, this service is readily available for you in Symfony, and all that you have to do in a service where you need to read annotations is to inject that annotation reader.

Let's define our annotation class as follows:

```
namespace Khepin\BookBundle\Security\Annotation;

/**
 * @Annotation
 */
class ValidateUser
{
    private $validation_group;
```

```
    public function __construct(array $parameters)
    {
        $this->validation_group = $parameters['value'];
    }

    public function getValidationGroup()
    {
        return $this->validation_group;
    }
}
```

The annotation is a simple value object containing the information that was passed to it, nothing more.

Let's try to read the annotation first to better understand how they work with regards to the reader by directly using it inside of our controller:

```
/**
 * @Route("/events/{event_id}/join")
 * @Template()
 * @ValidateUser("join_event")
 */
public function joinAction($event_id)
{
    $reader = $this->get('annotation_reader');
    $method = new \ReflectionMethod(
        get_class($this), 'joinAction');
    $annotation_name = 'Khepin\BookBundle\Security\
        Annotation\ValidateUser';
    $annotation = $reader->getMethodAnnotation(
        $method, $annotation_name);

    // ... Your normal code
}
```

We see that through our reader service, and by knowing only the name of the class and the method, we can read the annotation and get back an instance of our annotation class.

 Here, we create \ReflectionMethod directly because we already know the exact method we want to read an annotation for. You would probably, in most interesting cases, have to create a class named \ReflectionClass, and then loop over all defined methods to see which ones have the annotation you are looking for.

In the same way, you can read annotations for methods, properties, and the class itself, using the following code:

```
// Reading a class annotation
$reader->getClassAnnotation(
    new \ReflectionClass('MyClass'),
    '\My\Annotation'
);

// Reading a property annotation
$reader->getPropertyAnnotation(
    new \ReflectionProperty(
        'UserClass',
        'phone_number'
    ),
    '\My\Annotation'
);
```

The preceding code works well for reading a single annotation if you know which annotation you are looking for. For these cases, it is important to always use the fully qualified class name, including the namespace; otherwise, Doctrine's annotation reader will not be able to match the annotation class to the one you are trying to load.

For cases when you need to load all annotations and see which ones are defined, you can use get*Annotations() instead of the singular method. In this case, you would receive an array of all of the available annotations:

```
$annotation = $reader->getMethodAnnotations(
    new \ReflectionMethod(get_class($this), 'joinAction'));
=>
{
    [0]=> object(Sensio\Bundle\FrameworkExtraBundle\
        Configuration\Route),
    [1]=> object(Sensio\Bundle\FrameworkExtraBundle\
        Configuration\Template),
    [2]=> object(Khepin\BookBundle\Security\Annotation\
        ValidateUser)
}
```

 When adding annotations to entities or documents managed through Doctrine, you should not rely on get_class. Instead, use \Doctrine\Common\Util\ClassUtils::getClass because Doctrine will generate proxy classes for your entities, and in some cases, you will be trying to read the annotations on the proxy class instead of the class you are actually interested in. ClassUtils avoids this by returning the real class of an object instead of the proxy.

When a bundle is using annotations, it is creating a service in which the annotation reader is injected and then reads the annotation whenever needed. Even `SensioFrameworkExtraBundle`, which brings us the `@Route` and `@Template` annotations that we use on our `joinAction` method, does it the same way. By listening to the `kernel.controller` event before the controller is called, a service can read the required annotations and modify the behavior as needed.

> The annotation reader in Symfony will cache your annotations after they are read. Because PHP doesn't have support for annotations, they are created by adding comments. Parsing these comments on each request would be extremely slow. Make sure you use Symfony's `annotation_reader` service, and don't instantiate your own as it is already configured to speed things up and cache all read annotations.

Securing controllers with custom annotations

We now have all the building blocks in order to secure our actions, and we'll define a listener to the `kernel.controller` event:

```
security.access.valid_user:
    class:      Khepin\BookBundle\Security\ValidUserListener
    arguments: [@annotation_reader, @router, @session,
        @security.context, @validator]
    tags:
        - { name: kernel.event_listener,
        event: kernel.controller,
        method: onKernelController}
```

Our listener takes quite a few arguments. They are as follows:

- `annotation_reader`: This will allow us to read the arguments on each controller

- `router`: This will let us redirect the user to their profile page if their profile is not complete

- `session`: This is to add a "flash" message telling the user why they were redirected and what they have to do

- `security.context`: This is to retrieve the user

- `validator`: This is to validate the user

The controller event allows us to retrieve the controller in the form of an array:

```
{
    [0] => object('\My\Controller'),
    [1] => 'myAction'
}
```

This is everything we need in order to read our annotation. Now, change the controller as follows:

```
class ValidUserListener
{
    private $reader;

    private $router;

    private $session;

    private $sc;

    private $validator;

    private $annotation_name = 'Khepin\BookBundle\Security\
        Annotation\ValidateUser';

    public function __construct(Reader $reader, Router $router,
        Session $session, SecurityContext $sc,
            Validator $validator)
    {
        $this->reader = $reader;
        $this->router = $router;
        $this->session = $session;
        $this->sc = $sc;
        $this->validator = $validator;
    }

    public function onKernelController($event)
    {
        // Get class and method name to read the annotation
        $class_name = get_class($event->getController()[0]);
        $method_name = $event->getController()[1];

        $method = new \ReflectionMethod(
        $class_name, $method_name);
```

```
// Read the annotation
$annotation = $this->reader->getMethodAnnotation($method,
            $this->annotation_name);

// If our controller doesn't have a "ValidateUser"
// annotation, we don't do anything
if (!is_null($annotation)) {
    // Retrieve the validation group from the
    // annotation, and try to validate the user
    $validation_group = $annotation->getValidationGroup();
    $user = $this->sc->getToken()->getUser();
    $errors = $this->validator->validate($user,
        $validation_group);

    if (count($errors)) {
        // If the user is not valid, change the
        // controller to redirect the user
        $event->setController(function()
            {
                $this->session->getFlashBag()->add(
                    'warning', 'You must fill in your
                    phone number before joining a
                    meetup.');
                $url = $this->router->generate(
                    'fos_user_profile_edit');
                return new RedirectResponse($url);
            });
    }
}
```

When we change the controller, we define an anonymous function instead of the array. All that is required is to pass a callable, so you could also pass in a static method, another callable array, and so on.

If you have a user defined that does not have a phone number, whenever they try to view the page to join a meetup, they are redirected to their profile page with a message saying they should update their phone number. If the phone number is present, then they see the page as requested.

> Here, this is secure because viewing the form to join a meetup and submitting the form are both in the same action. If you were to separate them, then both calls would need to be secure as well.

Securing an API – an example

It is becoming a common practice to only have an API on your web server and not generate the page's HTML on the server but through JavaScript in a user's browser.

However, it is also common for developers to still use standard sessions and logins when the API is only there to serve their own website at first. This can lead to issues regarding security. Whenever you create a form to be displayed in Symfony via Twig, it contains a CSRF token. This token is here to help us ensure that not only is the request coming from this user's browser (cookies do that) but also from your actual webpage and not a malicious tab in the user's browser.

With an API, your forms are going to be generated entirely in the frontend. So, they cannot include a CSRF token. Furthermore, whenever an attacker submits a request to our server through a user's browser, all the cookies will be sent together, allowing the attacker to control the user's account. However, because of the same origin policy in browsers, an attacker's script cannot see what the cookies are for our website. So a technique to still defend ourselves is to double-submit the cookies, once normally, which we don't control, and once through a custom header.

An attacker will not be able to reproduce this, and for us, through the JavaScript that we are using, it is very easy to include this duplicated header on every request.

Since we are only checking for permissions and access, we create the simplest possible controller:

```
/**
 * @Route("/api/status")
 */
public function apiAction()
{
    return new Response('The API works great!');
}
```

Now, for any request to a URL starting with /api/, we want to make sure that our cookie exists twice. In the following code snippet, we will use events in a way similar to what we did with annotations earlier, but this time, we'll use the kernel.request event as it happens earlier. Also, in this case, we don't need information about the controller.

```
security.access.api:
    class:        Khepin\BookBundle\Security\ApiCustomCookieListener
    tags:
        - { name: kernel.event_listener,
          event: kernel.request,
          method: onKernelRequest }
```

This listener will receive the request through the event and only compare two headers of this request, so it will not require any argument. The listener is also very easy to implement:

```php
namespace Khepin\BookBundle\Security;

use Symfony\Component\HttpFoundation\Response;

class ApiCustomCookieListener
{
    public function onKernelRequest($event)
    {
        // We only secure urls in our API
        if (strpos(
      $event->getRequest()->getPathInfo(),
      '/api/'
          ) !== 0
        ) {
            return;
        }

        $cookie = $event->getRequest()->headers
        ->get('cookie');
        $double = $event->getRequest()->headers
        ->get('X-Doubled-Cookie');

        if ($cookie !== $double) {
            $event->setResponse(new Response('', 400));
        }
    }
}
```

With just these few lines, we have enabled the CSRF protection on an API with a cost that is a lot less than that of using CSRF tokens as compared to forms, as these need to be random and encrypted values.

Summary

Security is a huge topic and a source of endless debate. This chapter showed you how to craft authentication and authorization mechanisms in Symfony, but it's important to understand that security does not stop there. Depending on the level of security required by your application, you should always do your research on how to best make it safe for you and your users.

Although creating your own authentication method is a bit complex in Symfony, it's done in a way that is highly modular and customizable. For that reason, most authentication schemes you might encounter will already have an existing third party bundle that you could use, relieving you of the implementation effort.

We also saw how roles, ACLs, and voters can be used independently or together to give various authorizations to different users. Roles, combined with voters, allow for a powerful and expressive way to control access.

In the next chapter, we will take a break from Symfony to talk about Doctrine. Doctrine is not the only persistence layer that can be used, but it is Symfony's default choice and offers a lot in terms of extensibility.

5
Doctrine

Doctrine is the **Object-relational Mapper (ORM)** that ships with Symfony. It lets you work with PHP classes and objects, and handles their storage and retrieval to and from a data store. It can work with a variety of data stores such as traditional relational databases or document databases. The examples in this chapter will be either for the ORM or for the MongoDB **ODM (Object-document Mapper)**.

Creating your own data types

Not all databases are created equal! MongoDB can store a collection of values or documents within a document, which is impossible in most relational databases. PostgreSQL can deal with geographical values, but MySQL can't.

For this reason, Doctrine only ships with a subset of standard supported types that are common across most of the databases. But, what if you want to use features specific to your database vendor or invent your own form of mapping type? You can define these types in exactly the same way Doctrine does.

User and meetup locations

We have already created a class named Coordinates to hold the latitude and longitude of a meetup. We have also created a query in our first controller to get a user only the events within a 50 km side square centered on them. There are a few problems with this; firstly, we can only use a square (or force the DB to do some calculation on each row), and secondly, there's no index on these queries, so it might slow down after some time.

MongoDB has support for geospatial indexes, but it requires the locations to be stored as [latitude, longitude]. If we had used MongoDB instead of a relational database in the first place, our meetup class would look as follows:

```
/**
 * @ODM\Document
 */
class Meetup
{
    /**
     * @ODM\Id
     */
    protected $id;

    /**
     * @ODM\String
     */
    protected $name;

    /**
     * @ODM\???
     */
    protected $location;

    // Getters and Setters ...
}
```

The annotation for location is ??? as we don't know how to store this yet! So, we'll create our own Doctrine mapping type to be applied here. Let's say, we add a custom type named `coordinates`, and then our annotation will become as follows:

```
/**
 * @ODM\Field(type="coordinates")
 */
```

For Doctrine to become aware of our custom type, we need to do the following two things:

- Create the `Type` class
- Tell Doctrine about it

The `Type` class is very simple to understand, but there's a catch since some of its behavior is not yet implemented in Doctrine's ODM! It has the following four possible methods:

- `convertToPHPValue`
- `convertToDatabaseValue`
- `closureToPHP`
- `closureToDatabase`

The names are immediately easy to understand. The two `closureTo*` methods actually return a string containing PHP code that will be used during Doctrine's code generation. Here's the catch: `convertToPHPValue` doesn't work. It is simply never called, so you must use the `closureToPHP` method instead, as follows:

```php
namespace Khepin\BookBundle\Document;
use Doctrine\ODM\MongoDB\Types\Type;
use Doctrine\ODM\MongoDB\Types\DateType;
use Khepin\BookBundle\Geo\Coordinate;
use Symfony\Component\Validator\Exception\UnexpectedTypeException;

class CoordinatesType extends Type
{
    public function convertToPHPValue($value)
    {
        return new Coordinate($value[0], $value[1]);
    }

    public function convertToDatabaseValue($value)
    {
        if (!$value instanceof Coordinate) {
            throw new UnexpectedTypeException($value,
                'Khepin\BookBundle\Geo\Coordinate');
        }
        return [$value->getLatitude(), $value->getLongitude()];
    }

    public function closureToPHP()
    {
      return '$return = new
        \Khepin\BookBundle\Geo\Coordinate($value[0], $value[1]);';
    }
}
```

Also, be careful, because your closure's code will actually be written as code in a completely different context than the one of this class; therefore, it is important to use fully qualified namespaces.

In Doctrine's base type class, we find a list of all available types as a static array, as follows:

```
private static $typesMap = array(
    self::STRING => 'Doctrine\ODM\MongoDB\Types\StringType',
    self::DATE => 'Doctrine\ODM\MongoDB\Types\DateType',
    // ...
);
```

This is where our type must be declared for Doctrine to know about it. It is registered as follows:

```
use Doctrine\ODM\MongoDB\Types\Type;
Type::addType('coordinates',
    'Khepin\BookBundle\Document\CoordinatesType');
```

The Mongo ODM bundle doesn't offer a way (similar to forms) of tagging your types and letting Doctrine register them on its own. As the preceding two lines of code are only here to declare how to load a special type, we'll add them to app/autoload.php.

Testing

Let's test whether our mapping is working properly using the following code:

```
use Symfony\Bundle\FrameworkBundle\Test\WebTestCase;
use Khepin\BookBundle\Document\Meetup;
use Khepin\BookBundle\Geo\Coordinate;

class MongoCoordinateTypeTest extends WebTestCase
{
    public function testMapping()
    {
        $client = static::createClient();
        $dm = $client->getContainer()->get('doctrine.odm');
```

Create a new meetup with a unique name and persist it, as follows:

```
$meetup = new Meetup();
$name = uniqid();
$meetup->setName($name);
$meetup->setLocation(new Coordinate(33, 75));

$dm->persist($meetup);
$dm->flush();
```

We will retrieve our meetup through PHP's native Mongo extension, using the following code, to verify that the value was indeed stored as an array:

```
$m = new \MongoClient();
$db = $m->extending;
$collection = $db->Meetup;

$met = $collection->findOne(['name' => $name]);
$this->assertTrue(is_array($met['location']));
$this->assertTrue($met['location'][0] === 33);
```

We set a new value without Doctrine, directly by setting an array in the database as follows:

```
$newName = uniqid();
$collection->insert([
    'name' => $newName,
    'location' => [11, 22]
]);
```

Now, retrieve our meetup through Doctrine and verify that we get a coordinate, as follows:

```
$dbmeetup = $dm->getRepository('KhepinBookBundle:Meetup')-
    >findOneBy(['name' => $newName]);
$this->assertTrue($dbmeetup->getLocation() instanceof
    Coordinate);
}
```

Finally, test that the correct exception is thrown if we pass something that is not a coordinate, using the following code:

```
/**
 * @expectedException \Symfony\Component\Validator\Exception\
UnexpectedTypeException
 */
public function testTypeException()
{
    $client = static::createClient();
    $dm = $client->getContainer()->get('doctrine.odm');

    $name = uniqid();
    $meetup = new Meetup();
    $meetup->setName($name);
    $meetup->setLocation([1,2]);

    $dm->persist($meetup);
    $dm->flush();
}
```

Custom DQL functions

Doctrine can be adapted to many different database vendors such as MySQL, PostgreSQL, and others. To achieve this and still be able to take advantage of the specifics of each underlying platform, Doctrine is designed in such a way that it is easy to define your own custom SQL functions.

We will take advantage of this for our geolocation. In the first chapter, we decided that the home page would only display events within 25 kilometers (which roughly translates to 0.3 in terms of latitude and longitude). To do so, we defined a box of coordinates around a given point and then used it in the SQL code.

However, an actual distance between two points (in a Cartesian plan) is calculated by the following formula:

$$\sqrt{(x1 - x2)^2 + (y1 - y2)^2}$$

The preceding formula can be translated to the following SQL query:
SQRT (POW(lat_1 - lat_2, 2) + POW(long_1 - long_2, 2)).

This is correct; however, it is a bit tedious to write, so we'll take advantage of Doctrine's ability to define your own SQL functions and define a DISTANCE function that will be used as DISTANCE((lat_1, long_1), (lat_2, long_2)).

Let's go ahead and register it immediately in our config.yml file as follows:

```
orm:
    # ...
    dql:
        numeric_functions:
            distance: Khepin\BookBundle\Doctrine\DistanceFunction
```

The name we chose here, distance, is important. Doctrine will register it as an identifier so that whenever it encounters the word DISTANCE in our DQL, it will call our DistanceFunction to take over.

We will also update our controller code so that it uses this new DQL function as follows:

```
/**
 * @Route("/")
 * @Template()
 */
public function indexAction()
```

```php
{
    $position = $this->get('user_locator')->getUserCoordinates();
    $position = [
        'latitude' => $position->getLatitude(),
        'longitude' => $position->getLongitude()
    ];

    // Create our database query
    $em = $this->getDoctrine()->getManager();

    $qb = $em->createQueryBuilder();
    $qb->select('e')
        ->from('KhepinBookBundle:Event', 'e')
        ->where('DISTANCE((e.latitude, e.longitude), (:latitude,
            :longitude)) < 0.3')
        ->setParameters($position)
    ;

    // Retrieve interesting events
    $events = $qb->getQuery()->execute();

    return compact('events');
}
```

We can now define our new SQL function as follows:

```php
namespace Khepin\BookBundle\Doctrine;

use Doctrine\ORM\Query\AST\Functions\FunctionNode;
use Doctrine\ORM\Query\SqlWalker;
use Doctrine\ORM\Query\Parser;
use Doctrine\ORM\Query\Lexer;

class DistanceFunction extends FunctionNode
{
    protected $from = [];

    protected $to = [];

    public function parse(Parser $parser)
    {
        // ...
    }

    public function getSql(SqlWalker $sqlWalker)
    {
        // ...
    }
}
```

We have already stated that Doctrine should hand over the parsing to us whenever it encounters the DISTANCE token. Our function then needs to do the following two things:

- Parse the following DQL by consuming the DQL string until the final parenthesis of our DISTANCE function

- Generate some SQL, which will be the Cartesian distance calculation: SQRT(...)

Parsing the DQL is done by using the parser (which consumes the string), and the lexer, which knows how to read it.

When the parser *consumes* a part of the string, that part of the string is no longer available to be parsed by default. The parser advances its position in the string until the end, so we always need to be careful until which point we should parse the DQL.

The lexer knows about special DQL tokens such as parenthesis, commas, DQL function identifiers, and much more. By using these two, we tell the parser about our distance function in a way that can be described as follows:

```
Start with the **DISTANCE** identifier.
Find a **(**
    Find another **(**
        Find some expression (this could be a value, or a full SQL
select statement)
        Find a **,**
        Find some expression
    Find a **)**

    Find a **,**

    Find a **(**
        Find some expression
        Find a **,**
        Find some expression
    Find a **)**
Find a **)**
```

Our parse function actually looks very similar to the following few lines of code:

```
public function parse(Parser $parser)
{
    // Match: DISTANCE( (lat, long), (lat, long))
    $parser->match(Lexer::T_IDENTIFIER);
    $parser->match(Lexer::T_OPEN_PARENTHESIS);
```

```
        // First (lat, long)
        $parser->match(Lexer::T_OPEN_PARENTHESIS);
            $this->from['latitude'] = $parser
                ->ArithmeticPrimary();
            $parser->match(Lexer::T_COMMA);
            $this->from['longitude'] = $parser
                ->ArithmeticPrimary();
        $parser->match(Lexer::T_CLOSE_PARENTHESIS);

        $parser->match(Lexer::T_COMMA);

        // Second (lat, long)
        $parser->match(Lexer::T_OPEN_PARENTHESIS);
            $this->to['latitude'] = $parser
                ->ArithmeticPrimary();
            $parser->match(Lexer::T_COMMA);
            $this->to['longitude'] = $parser
                ->ArithmeticPrimary();
        $parser->match(Lexer::T_CLOSE_PARENTHESIS);

    $parser->match(Lexer::T_CLOSE_PARENTHESIS);
}
```

We will save the matched expressions as a `from` and `to` variable so that we can use them to generate the SQL later.

It is possible to check what the next token will be without consuming it to provide different possible syntax of your DQL function through on of:

- `$parser->getLexer()->peek();`
- `$parser->getLexer()->glimpse();`
- `$parser->getLexer()->isNextToken(<token_type>);`

So, we can, for example, use both `DISTANCE( (lat, long), (lat, long) )` and `DISTANCE ( e, (lat, long) )` functions if we know that the selected element `e` has a latitude and longitude property.

If the parser does not find what it is supposed to, it will throw a syntax error. The code to generate the SQL statement then looks as follows:

```
public function getSql(SqlWalker $sqlWalker)
{
    $db = $sqlWalker->getConnection()->getDatabasePlatform();
    $sql = 'POW(%s - %s, 2) + POW(%s - %s, 2)';
```

```
$sql = sprintf(
    $sql,
    $this->from['latitude']->dispatch($sqlWalker),
    $this->to['latitude']->dispatch($sqlWalker),
    $this->from['longitude']->dispatch($sqlWalker),
    $this->to['longitude']->dispatch($sqlWalker)
);

$sql = $db->getSqrtExpression($sql);

return $sql;
}
```

 We could have written our SQL as SQRT (POW(%s - %s, 2) + POW(%s - %s, 2)) as the SQRT function is the same across all the major SQL database vendors. However, it is safer to rely on **Doctrines Database Abstraction Layer** to take care of these differences for us. As the POW function is not being included as an abstracted function, we can directly output its SQL statement.

What we stored in our `from` and `to` variables were not the results of SQL statements but the pieces of yet unparsed DQL. Since these could be anything from a literal value to a full SELECT statement, we can use the SQL Walker to keep generating the correct SQL for these expressions.

All Doctrine functions that you are currently using are also built this way, so you can find a lot of examples on how to write these functions within the Doctrine source code itself.

Versioning

A common issue when a lot of users have access to modifying the same resources is to make sure that they are not overwriting each other's changes. One technique to prevent this from happening is to version the resources. In Doctrine, we can set a version number to any entity when we first persist it, and then increment it whenever there is a request to change the information.

This will allow us to check if the version number of the incoming request is at least equal to the current one in the database. If not, refuse the change and force the user to refresh before updating the content.

Doctrine also uses events that we can listen to. These are as follows:

- `prePersist`: This event is triggered before the entity is persisted to the database for the first time.

- `preRemove`: This event occurs before deleting an object.

- `preUpdate`: This event occurs before a new version of the entity is saved to the database.

- `post*`: All the preceding events also have a post version that occurs after the action has been completed.

- `postLoad`: This event is triggered after loading data from the database.

- `pre / on / postFlush`: These events are not tied to a single entity, but occur when the entity manager is performing actions on the database.

- `onClear`: This event occurs when the entity manager has no more work to do on the entities.

- `loadClassMetadata`: This event is triggered when Doctrine has loaded metadata such as the mapping information about a class. This can be useful if you need to create a service that knows about different entity relations in your application.

Using these events, it is possible to add behavior to your entities and share this behavior among them. Some famous use cases include creating a soft delete behavior where a `delete` flag is set to `true` instead of actually removing the information from the database, dynamically creating a URL-friendly version of an article's title, saving the time of creation and last update, and so on.

To make it easy to share our `Versionable` behavior, we'll add the required fields and methods in a `Trait` method, as follows:

```
namespace Khepin\BookBundle\Doctrine;
use Doctrine\ORM\Mapping as ORM;

Trait Versionable
{
    /**
     * @ORM\Column(name="version", type="integer", length=255)
     * @ORM\Version
     */
    private $version;

    public function getVersion()
    {
```

```
        return $this->version;
    }

    public function setVersion($version)
    {
        $this->version = $version;
    }
}
```

This way, all we have to do for an entity, such as our meetups, to become versionable is to add the trait as follows:

```
class Event
{
    use Versionable;
    // ...
}
```

> The @ORM\Version annotation indicates to Doctrine that this field is to be used to compare versions. Doctrine doesn't provide a versionable trait but gives you the tools to create your own so that your version property can be an integer, a timestamp, a hashed value of the entity, and so on.

We identified two important steps in our process; first, we set a version number of 1 whenever the entity is created, and secondly, we used it to verify the validity of an operation and incremented it.

Setting a version on all entities

Since we are going to use listeners and events, we will again define a service as follows:

```
khepin.doctrine.versionable:
    class: Khepin\BookBundle\Doctrine\VersionableListener
    tags:
        - { name: doctrine.event_listener, event: prePersist }
        - { name: doctrine.event_listener, event: preUpdate }
```

We have already set our service to listen to both the prePersist and preUpdate methods. In this case, we don't have to define a method to be called on the listener whenever the event is triggered. Doctrine will just call the prePersist method or the preUpdate method of the class.

Our listener is quite simple this time, so the service doesn't rely on any other service, but for each entity, if you wanted to add the name of the last person who updated it, then your service could depend on the security context in order to get the current connected user.

 Although it is tempting to define Doctrine extensions that integrate with Symfony services in such a way, especially for adding the user, you should use this with caution and make sure that your code is flexible enough. Whenever you want to manipulate your objects from the command line, your listener might be called, but the user session or the security context would not exist, and this will prevent you from performing useful database operations from a command line.

In order to just set the version on any entity, it's quite easy. We only do it through the listener to show how it is working; otherwise, simply setting a default value of 1, as follows, would have been perfectly fine:

```php
<?php
namespace Khepin\BookBundle\Doctrine;

use Doctrine\ORM\Event\LifecycleEventArgs;

class VersionableListener {
    public function prePersist(LifecycleEventArgs $args)
    {
        $entity = $args->getEntity();

        $versionable = in_array(
            'Khepin\BookBundle\Doctrine\Versionable',
            (new \ReflectionClass($entity))->getTraitNames()
        );

        if ($versionable) {
            $entity->setVersion(1);
        }
    }
}
```

The listener will be called for absolutely all entities before it is persisted, no matter if we added the Versionable trait or not. So, the first thing to do is check that we are dealing with an object that we actually want to version. We do this by verifying that our class uses the Versionable trait.

If we need to update the version, then we set it to 1.

Using and updating versions

Now, when we are about to save an updated object, we must check whether it is
versionable, check whether the current version is compared to the database value,
decide to allow the update or not, and increment the version number, by using the
following code:

```
public function preUpdate(LifecycleEventArgs $args)
{
  $entity = $args->getEntity();
  $em = $args->getEntityManager();

  $versionable = in_array(
    'Khepin\BookBundle\Doctrine\Versionable',
    (new \ReflectionClass($entity))->getTraitNames()
  );

  if ($versionable) {
    $em->lock(
      $entity,
      LockMode::OPTIMISTIC,
      $entity->getVersion()
    );
    $version = $entity->getVersion();
    $uow = $em->getUnitOfWork();
    $uow->propertyChanged(
      $entity,
      'version',
      $version,
      $version + 1
    );
  }
}
```

Since we added the @ORM\Version annotation to our Trait earlier, we can take
advantage of Doctrine's entity locking. The OPTIMISTIC lock is one of the defaults
that come with Doctrine. When we try to lock the entity, if the version number
present in the database is not the same as the one present in the entity (someone
else modified it in the meantime), Doctrine will throw an exception and the entity
cannot be updated.

Notice that we have to then explicitly tell the **unit of work** that the version was
updated. A unit of work is a small set of all the changes that the entity manager has
to perform when $em->flush() is called. It already contains the newly computed
values ready to be saved to the database. Here, since it has already been computed,
we need to explicitly let it know that there is a new value.

Testing

Testing anything directly related to Doctrine like this is usually easier and is better done by directly interacting with the database. Therefore, your tests will modify the data included in the database. This might not be what you want if you cannot set up a clean test environment. One way to do it is to redefine the Doctrine connection for the test environment and use `sqlite`. This can be done in the `config_test.yml` file, as follows:

```
doctrine:
    dbal:
        driver:    pdo_sqlite
        host:      localhost
        port:      null
        dbname:    test_db
        user:      root
        password:  null
        charset:   UTF8
        path: %kernel.root_dir%/.../ BookBundle/Tests/db.sqlite
```

As long as you are running tests, you will be in the test environment, and any call to `$container->get('doctrine')` will return a connection to the `test` database. If you wish to execute any command in that environment (to first create the DB and schema, for example), just execute your normal command and add `--env test`.

Other than that, our tests are pretty simple and straightforward:

```
class VersionableTest extends WebTestCase
{
    public function testVersionAdded()
    {
        $client = static::createClient();

        $meetup = new Event();
        $em = $client->getContainer()->get('doctrine')->getManager();

        $this->assertTrue($meetup->getVersion() === null);

        $em->persist($meetup);
        $em->flush();

        $em->refresh($meetup);

        $this->assertTrue($meetup->getVersion() === 1);
    }
```

```php
/**
 * @expectedException \Exception
 */
public function testRefuseOutdated()
{
    $client = static::createClient();
    $meetup = new Event();
    $em = $client->getContainer()->get('doctrine')
                    ->getManager();
    $em->persist($meetup);
    $em->flush();

    $meetup->setName('myEvent');
    $meetup->setVersion(0);
    $em->flush();
}

public function testIncrementedVersion()
{
    $client = static::createClient();
    $meetup = new Event();
    $em = $client->getContainer()->get('doctrine')
            ->getManager();
    $em->persist($meetup);
    $em->flush();

    $this->assertTrue($meetup->getVersion() === 1);

    $em->refresh($meetup);
    $meetup->setName('test event');
    $em->flush();
    $this->assertTrue($meetup->getVersion() == 2);
}
}
```

Creating a Doctrine filter

With the two types of extensions we already saw, a lot can be done. We could create an extension that notifies us whenever an entity has been updated, by whom, or create URL-friendly names for entities. We know how to deal with entity versions; we could even extend that behavior to save all the previous versions of an entity and maintain a record history. Some behaviors, though, can still not be achieved with what we have seen.

If we want, we can create a soft delete, or ensure automatically that all database queries include `user_id` so that a user can see only data that belongs to them. In the latter case, we will be able to easily add a value to a `user_id` field on any entity before it is persisted, but while retrieving entities through a SQL query, we still need to remember to add the `user_id = "123"` value every time we write a query. This is likely to be forgotten, and that can cause some big issues, because your app will start to leak data from one user to another.

A better version will be that all queries have this bit of logic added automatically. In Doctrine, before version 2.2, you would have had to create a custom AST Walker. The **AST (Abstract Syntax Tree) Walker** is the class that generates the actual SQL statement based on the query you have defined in the query builder. The query builder receives chunks of SQL statements when you use the following code:

```
$qb->select('u')
    ->from('User', 'u')
    ->where('u.id = ?1')
    ->orderBy('u.name', 'ASC');
```

This was a bit complex and inconvenient.

Doctrine 2.2 and higher versions came with the concept of filters that allow you to do exactly this. Filters also come with the advantage that they can easily be enabled and disabled, so whenever you are writing commands for doing administrative work on your database, you can completely bypass the filter and perform your normal work.

We will first configure and add a very simple filter class by adding a filters entry to the ORM configuration, as follows:

```
orm:
    auto_generate_proxy_classes: %kernel.debug%
    auto_mapping: true
    filters:
        - { name: owner_filter, class:
          Khepin\BookBundle\Doctrine\OwnerFilter, enabled:
            true }
```

Sadly, it is not possible to use a service as a filter. Doctrine registers filters by class name. So, we won't be able to inject the current user inside of the filter. We also need to remember that the filter will be applied to *all* queries, even the one that retrieves our user from the database. So, we need a way to differentiate between entities for which this filter should be applied and those for which it is not needed.

We will define a simple PHP interface (an empty one) that will allow us to make the distinction between entities to which the filter should be applied and others. As with security, the secure option should always be the default one. It is better to pull your hair for an hour because you don't understand where this user_id = 123 constraint is coming from in your SQL statement, rather than having the user data exposed wrongly because you forgot to add a UserOwnedEntity interface to a specific entity.

To be on the safe side, we use the opposite of the UserOwnedEntity interface, as follows:

```
// Interface
namespace Khepin\BookBundle\Doctrine;

interface NonUserOwnedEntity
{

}

// Filter
namespace Khepin\BookBundle\Doctrine;
use Doctrine\ORM\Mapping\ClassMetaData,
    Doctrine\ORM\Query\Filter\SQLFilter;

class OwnerFilter extends SQLFilter
{
    public function addFilterConstraint(ClassMetadata $targetEntity,
      $targetTableAlias)
    {
        if ($targetEntity->reflClass->implementsInterface('Khepin\
          BookBundle\Doctrine\NonUserOwnedEntity')) {
            return "";
        }

        return $targetTableAlias.'.user_id = ' . $this-
          >getParameter('user_id');
    }
}
```

We also need to remember that before any user is logged in, it is impossible to have the proper parameter value.

Doctrine allows us to retrieve the filters later, so we can still use an event listener that will be triggered on each request once the user information is available, and pass the correct parameter at that point. We will also disable our filter before this happens since the database will be queried at least once to get the current user information. This will prevent some future mistakes.

Our `OwnerFilter` class doesn't need to change except in the configuration where we will now set it to `enable: false` by default. We'll need to create an event listener that:

- Knows the user (inject `@security.context`)
- Knows about Doctrine (inject `@doctrine`)
- Is triggered very early on each request (listen to `kernel.request`)

`kernel.request` is the first event that gets triggered for any request, and it is called on every request. If the user previously logged in, the user information is already present when the `kernel.request` event is triggered. The following code shows the use of the `kernel.request` event:

```
khepin.doctrine.owned_entity.listener:
    class: Khepin\BookBundle\Doctrine\OwnerListener
    arguments: [@doctrine, @security.context]
    tags:
        - { name: kernel.event_listener, event: kernel.request
          , method: updateFilter }
```

The event listener class itself isn't very complex, as shown in the following code:

```php
namespace Khepin\BookBundle\Doctrine;

class OwnerListener
{
    private $em;
    private $security_context;

    public function __construct($doctrine, $security_context)
    {
        $this->em = $doctrine->getManager();
        $this->security_context = $security_context;
    }

    public function updateFilter()
    {
        $id = $this->security_context->getToken()->getUser()-
            >getUserId();
        $this->em->getFilters()->enable('owner_filter')-
            >setParameter('user_id', $id);
    }
}
```

Summary

This chapter covered a great deal of what you could want to do in using and extending Doctrine. Combining events and filters, you can create very solid extensions. Do you want to create a new CMS where articles can only be seen after they are "published"? Events and filters will come along nicely to provide a publishable behavior to your entities. Do you need to keep versions of all changes and know who made what change and when? Here again, the events will allow you to have this taken care of on all entities without worrying about manually doing it.

As an exercise, you can try to implement a soft delete behavior. Soft delete indicates that whenever an entity is about to be deleted, you instead update a deleted field to true, or to the timestamp at which it was deleted. Creating a `SoftDeleteable` behavior for your entities should involve both listening to events and using a filter.

I mentioned earlier about Doctrine's Abstract Syntax Tree and how it used to be necessary before Doctrine added the concept of filters. There are still cases where you might want to use these, for example to augment the DQL syntax or to tailor it to your specific database vendor.

With all this, you are now fully equipped to create any type of extension in Symfony. But, the whole point of creating an extension rather than just coding something that works in one place is to be able to reuse and share it. In the last chapter, we will take a look at the possibilities to do so in Symfony.

6
Sharing Your Extensions

Since everything is a bundle in Symfony, all the code you write is already in the structure it needs to be in order to be shared with others. If we take all the code that we wrote over the course of this book inside the `BookBundle` folder, and make it available to others, all they would have to do to make it work is copy our configurations. This is nice, but it is still a "lot of work" to do, which includes defining each of the services with the right parameters and so on.

In this chapter, we will look at the steps required to make an easy-to-use bundle for others as well as other best practices for sharing code. In *Chapter 4*, *Security*, we added a way for users to sign in using their GitHub account. This is a good example of something that others might want to reuse or that we ourselves might want to reuse from one project to another.

Creating the bundle

While developing our app initially, we didn't care about where our files were. Everything was under a giant monolithic bundle that included everything. We'll go through the following steps to change the situation and make a decoupled `GithubAuthBundle`:

1. Set up the bundle.
2. Move or write the code.
3. Move or create the services configuration directly in the bundle.
4. Define the bundle configuration and merge the user-defined parameters.

First, we will use the following command line provided by Symfony to generate an empty bundle:

```
php app/console generate:bundle
```

To do this, you have to choose a namespace and a bundle name, which in the case of this book are Khepin and GithubAuthBundle. Now, let's move all the required files to this new bundle and update their namespaces accordingly. In the end, our bundle structure should be as follows:

```
GithubAuthBundle/
    DependencyInjection/
        Configuration.php
        KhepinGithubAuthExtension.php
    Resources/
        config/
            services.xml
    Security/
        Github/
            AuthenticationListener.php
            AuthenticationProvider.php
            GithubUserToken.php
            SecurityFactory.php
            UserProvider.php
    Test/
    KhepinGithubAuthBundle.php
```

Also note that the KhepinGitAuthBundle bundle class now needs to contain the code that was previously in KhepinBookBundle to register the security factory, as follows:

```php
// Updated BookBundle class
namespace Khepin\BookBundle;

use Symfony\Component\HttpKernel\Bundle\Bundle;

class KhepinBookBundle extends Bundle
{
}

// GithubAuthBundle class
namespace Khepin\GithubAuthBundle;
```

```
use Symfony\Component\HttpKernel\Bundle\Bundle;
use Symfony\Component\DependencyInjection\ContainerBuilder;
use Khepin\GithubAuthBundle\Security\Github\SecurityFactory;

class KhepinGithubAuthBundle extends Bundle
{
    public function build(ContainerBuilder $container)
    {
        parent::build($container);

        $extension = $container->getExtension('security');
        $extension->addSecurityListenerFactory(
        new SecurityFactory()
        );
    }
}
```

Once we do so, our previously working code will stop functioning. All the services we had defined in our `config.yml` file are now referencing the files that are not there anymore.

Symfony lets us move the service definitions to the bundles themselves. This is what we will do, going from a YML-based configuration to an XML-based one. It is recommended that you use XML when creating a bundle to be shared with others instead of other forms of configurations (PHP, annotations, or YML) since the XML format is more flexible.

Our initial configuration is as follows:

```
khepin.github.authentication_provider:
    class: Khepin\BookBundle\Security\Github\AuthenticationProvider
    public: false
```

Now, the configuration is different, as follows:

```
<service
    id="khepin.github.authentication_provider"
    class="Khepin\GithubAuthBundle\Security\ …
        … Github\AuthenticationProvider"
    public="false">
</service>
```

The complete configuration of the file is as follows:

```xml
<?xml version="1.0" ?>

<container xmlns="http://symfony.com/schema/dic/services"
    xmlns:xsi="http://www.w3.org/2001/XMLSchema-instance"
    xsi:schemaLocation="http://symfony.com/schema/dic/services
        http://symfony.com/schema/dic/services/services-1.0.xsd">

    <services>
        <service
            id="khepin.github.authentication_provider"
            class="Khepin\GithubAuthBundle\Security\Github\ …
            … AuthenticationProvider"
            public="false">
        </service>
        <service
            id="khepin.github.user_provider"
            class="Khepin\GithubAuthBundle\Security\ …
            … Github\UserProvider">
            <argument type="service"
                    id="fos_user.user_manager" />
        </service>
        <service
            id="khepin.github.authentication_listener"
            class="Khepin\GithubAuthBundle\Security\ …
        … Github\AuthenticationListener"
            parent="security.authentication.listener.abstract"
            abstract="true"
            public="false">
        </service>
    </services>
</container>
```

Our bundle is now self contained, and no configuration will be needed to make it work in another project. However, you will still need to add the bundle to the AppKernel file, and set up the user provider in the security configuration.

Exposing the configuration

There is a problem with our AuthenticationListener class though. From where we left things in *Chapter 4, Security*, it contained the credentials for our GitHub application. We'll want our users to provide their own credentials instead.

The `AuthenticationListener` class is as follows:

```
class AuthenticationListener extends AbstractAuthenticationListener
{
    protected $client_id;

    protected $client_secret;

    protected function attemptAuthentication(Request $request)
    {
        $client = new \Guzzle\Http\Client(
        'https://github.com/login/oauth/access_token'
        );
        $req = $client->post('', null, [
            'client_id' => $this->client_id,
            'client_secret' => $$this->client_secret,
            'code' => $request->query->get('code')
        ])->setHeader('Accept', 'application/json');
        // ...
    }

    public function setClientId($id)
    {
        $this->client_id = $id;
    }

    public function setClientSecret($secret)
    {
        $this->client_secret = $secret;
    }
}
```

We will update our `AuthenticationListener` class to provide two methods to set the credentials. We know that since our class inherits from an abstract class, the constructor methods within that class take many parameters and are already configured. We prefer to avoid messing with this as there is a risk of breaking compatibility if the underlying interface changes in the future. For this, we will inject the following arguments through methods instead of the constructor:

```
<service
    id="khepin.github.authentication_listener"
    class="Khepin\GithubAuthBundle\Security\Github\ …
        … AuthenticationListener"
    parent="security.authentication.listener.abstract"
```

```
        abstract="true"
        public="false">
        <call method="setClientId">
            <argument>xxxx</argument>
        </call>
        <call method="setClientSecret">
            <argument>xxxx</argument>
        </call>
    </service>
```

Now, we want to let other users configure these values from their own config.yml file as follows:

```
khepin_github_auth:
    client_id:      xxxx
    client_secret:  xxxx
```

To do this, we will update the services.xml service definition as follows:

```xml
<?xml version="1.0" ?>

<container xmlns="http://symfony.com/schema/dic/services"
    xmlns:xsi="http://www.w3.org/2001/XMLSchema-instance"
    xsi:schemaLocation="http://symfony.com/schema/dic/services
    http://symfony.com/schema/dic/services/services-1.0.xsd">

    <parameters>
        <parameter key="khepin_github_auth.client_id">
        </parameter>
        <parameter key="khepin_github_auth.client_secret">
        </parameter>
        <parameter
            key="khepin_github_auth.authentication_
                provider_class">
            Khepin\GithubAuthBundle\Security\Github\
                AuthenticationProvider
        </parameter>
        <parameter
            key="khepin_github_auth.user_provider_class">
                Khepin\GithubAuthBundle\Security\Github\
                    UserProvider
        </parameter>
        <parameter
            key="khepin_github_auth.authentication_
                listener_class">
```

```
                Khepin\GithubAuthBundle\Security\Github\
                    AuthenticationListener
            </parameter>
        </parameters>

        <services>
            <service
                id="khepin.github.authentication_provider"
                class="%khepin_github_auth. …
                … authentication_provider_class%"

                public="false">
            </service>
            <service
                id="khepin.github.user_provider"
                class="%khepin_github_auth.user_provider_class%">
                <argument type="service"
                    id="fos_user.user_manager" />
            </service>
            <service
                id="khepin.github.authentication_listener"
                class="%khepin_github_auth.authentication_
                    listener_class%"
                parent="security.authentication.listener.abstract"
                abstract="true"
                public="false">
                <call method="setClientId">
                <argument>
                    %khepin_github_auth.client_id%
                </argument>
                </call>
                <call method="setClientSecret">
                <argument>
                    %khepin_github_auth.client_secret%
                </argument>
                </call>
            </service>
        </services>
    </container>
```

The preceding code defines the `client_id` and `client_secret` parameters as well as three others for our implementation classes. It is usually a good practice to define these classnames as parameters. This will allow users to replace your implementation with another one if they need to later on. Those classes are defined with a value, so they don't need to be configured by default. The only parameters that are absolutely necessary are `client_id` and `client_secret`.

To load and validate the configuration of your bundle, you need to perform the following three steps:

1. Define the configuration format.
2. Load your XML configuration.
3. Merge it with the user-defined configuration.

When you create a bundle through the Symfony `generate` command, you will usually have a `DependencyInjection` folder in your bundle. This folder is here exactly for our purpose. It should contain the following two files:

- `Configuration.php`: This is the file where you define the structure of your configuration

- `Extension.php`: This is the file where you map the bundle and user-defined configuration together

The `Configuration.php` file contains the following lines of code:

```php
// Configuration.php
class Configuration implements ConfigurationInterface
{
    public function getConfigTreeBuilder()
    {
        $treeBuilder = new TreeBuilder();
        $rootNode = $treeBuilder->root('khepin_github_auth');

        $rootNode
            ->children()
            ->scalarNode('client_id')
            ->isRequired()->cannotBeEmpty()->end()
            ->scalarNode('client_secret')
            ->isRequired()->cannotBeEmpty()->end()
            ->scalarNode('authentication_provider_class')->end()
            ->scalarNode('user_provider_class')->end()
            ->scalarNode('authentication_listener_class')->end()
            ->end();

        return $treeBuilder;
    }
}
```

We have defined `client_id` and `client_secret` as two mandatory parameters for our configuration. We have also declared that our entire specific configuration should be under the `khepin_github_auth` key. This configuration class defines a specific tree structure that your configuration should stick to. This definition can get much more complex than the current one if, for example, you create multiple configurations of an object. If we wanted to configure multiple entity managers in Doctrine, it would require an array node instead of a scalar one. A simplified version of the code looks as follows:

```
$node = $treeBuilder->root('entity_managers');
$node
    ->requiresAtLeastOneElement()
    ->useAttributeAsKey('name')
    ->prototype('array')
        ->addDefaultsIfNotSet()
        ->children()
            ->scalarNode('connection')->end()
            ->scalarNode('class_metadata_factory_name')
                ->defaultValue('xxx')->end()
            ->scalarNode('default_repository_class')
                ->defaultValue('xxx')->end()
            ->scalarNode('auto_mapping')
                ->defaultFalse()->end()
            ->scalarNode('naming_strategy')
                ->defaultValue('xxx')->end()
            ->scalarNode('entity_listener_resolver')
                ->defaultNull()->end()
            ->scalarNode('repository_factory')
                ->defaultNull()->end()
        ->end()
    ->end()
;
```

The actual version in `DoctrineBundle` is a lot longer than this one, but this gives an idea of what is possible. Explaining all the details of what is possible through this configuration file would take a chapter of its own, and it might not be a very interesting one to read. It is possible to set information and examples for each node, validate their type and value, and so on. If you need something more advanced than the simple example here, for the bundle you are building, the best way to learn is to check the core Symfony bundles. They often allow some deep customization and, therefore, have pretty advanced configuration classes.

With this configuration class defined, we know that the configuration we get from the user is formatted properly and can be loaded by our extension class as follows:

```
class KhepinGithubAuthExtension extends Extension
{
    private $namespace = 'khepin_github_auth';

    public function load(array $configs, ContainerBuilder $container)
    {
        $configuration = new Configuration();
        $config = $this->processConfiguration(
            $configuration,
            $configs
        );

        $loader = new Loader\XmlFileLoader(
        $container,
        new FileLocator(__DIR__.'/../Resources/config')
        );
        $loader->load('services.xml');

        $this->setParameters(
            $container,
            $config, $this->namespace
        );
    }

    public function setParameters($container, $config, $ns)
    {
        foreach ($config as $key => $value) {
            $container->setParameter(
            $ns . '.' . $key,
            $value
            );
        }
    }
}
```

Most of this file would actually be generated for you. An interesting method is setParameters, which we have defined as a helper method. It takes the parameters in the user config, prefixes them with our configuration namespace, and sets the parameter's value as a container parameter. There is no official convention and nothing is enforced by Symfony regarding how you name your parameters, so this notion of namespace with all our parameters prefixed by khepin_github_ auth is just for convenience. However, it is not required in any way. Now, all our parameters are correctly set from app/config.yml, which lets the users of our bundle use it in a very simple way.

In a DEV environment, Symfony checks for file changes to see if it needs to reload and revalidate the configuration. This has a high performance cost, so it is not enabled in a PROD environment, where the configuration will be parsed once and cached for later use.

Getting ready to share

With the changes made to the bundle earlier, your bundle is technically ready to be shared between various projects. However, what's left to do? It all depends on your goals, but if you went through all the trouble to create a reusable bundle, maybe even an open source one for all the world to use, then you don't want your efforts to be vain, and you hope that many people will start using your bundle. To improve the adoption and usefulness of your bundles, here's what you should always do.

Research

KNP Labs, a very active company in the Symfony community, created a website (http://knpbundles.com) that lists many Symfony bundles and gives them a score based on popularity, recommendations, activity, testing status, and so on.

A simple search on this website will show us at least two existing bundles for performing authentication through GitHub. It is possible that you have a specific need that is not addressed by these bundles, but in that case, you would do the Symfony community a better service by contacting the author of one of these bundles and trying to improve their work together. One bundle with two authors that fits more (still related) use cases is better and more useful in general than two bundles with a 90 percent functionality overlap and 10 percent specificity.

Documentation

So, your bundle is now available on the Web. It has been indexed on knpbundles as well and people can start using it. There are two kinds of bundles that your fellow developers enjoy or agree to use: the ones that are done so well and have such a clear API that they don't require any documentation to be used (let's settle for very little documentation) and the ones with a clear and extensive documentation. In our case, you can simply add a README file to the bundle, mentioning what it does (user authentication through GitHub), what it needs (FOSUserBundle is a prerequisite), how to install it, and how to configure it.

If your bundle becomes much bigger, think about setting up a small web page for a clearer documentation. The GitHub pages can be very useful here.

Testing

Many people will refuse (with reason) to use a bundle that is not properly tested. There are services (such as `Travic.CI`) that will let you run the test suite on every single commit you make to your bundle. They will provide you with a little badge to include in your documentation, which will tell the world whether your tests are currently successful or not.

When you are testing a bundle independently of the framework, you don't benefit as much from all the configuration and setup that Symfony does for you. If you have doubts on how you should write your tests or configure a specific service for your tests, it's always a good idea to learn from other bundles that deal with similar problems and gain knowledge from the way they do things.

Let's add some testing to our bundle. First, we make use of a composer to define what libraries we will be using for testing as well as how to autoload our bundle classes. This is done through the `autoload`, `target-dir` and `require-dev` sections of `composer.json`. The reference to the full `composer.json` file can be found in the following *Distribution and licensing* section.

In the `Tests` folder, we create the following two files:

- `phpunit.xml`: This file configures `phpunit`
- `bootstrap.php`: This file will hold any bootstrapping code that you might need before running your tests, such as configuring a Doctrine connection and mappings, wiring up complex services, and so on

The most basic `phpunit` configuration will be as follows:

```xml
<?xml version="1.0" encoding="UTF-8"?>
<phpunit bootstrap="bootstrap.php">
    <testsuites>
        <testsuite name="Github Authentication">
            <directory suffix=".php">./</directory>
        </testsuite>
    </testsuites>
</phpunit>
```

This defines one test suite and tells `phpunit` to execute `bootstrap.php` before running any tests.

Remember that phpunit is only one of the possible options for unit testing your bundle. This is the one we use in this book as it is the default one in Symfony, but now, more and more bundles have their tests using different tools such as **Atoum** (http://atoum.org) or **phpspec** (http://www.phpspec.net/). For example, the following snippet makes use of **Mockery** (https://github.com/padraic/mockery) as a replacement for the mocks of phpunit.

Once we have set up our configuration, it is possible to add the first test as follows:

```
use Khepin\GithubAuthBundle\Security\Github
                    \AuthenticationProvider;
use \Mockery as m;

class AuthenticationProviderTest extends \PHPUnit_Framework_TestCase
{
    public function testAuthenticatesToken()
    {
        $user = m::mock(['getName' => 'Molly',
                    'getRoles' => ['ROLE_ADMIN']]);
        $user_provider = m::mock(['loadOrCreateUser' => $user]);
        $unauthenticated_token = m::mock(
          'Khepin\GithubAuthBundle\Security\Github\GithubUserToken',
          ['getCredentials' => 'molly@example.com']);
        $auth_provider = new AuthenticationProvider(
            $user_provider);
        $token = $auth_provider
            ->authenticate($unauthenticated_token);
        $this->assertTrue($token->isAuthenticated());
        $this->assertEquals($token->getUser()->getName(),'Molly');
    }
}
```

Distribution and licensing

Symfony makes heavy use of composer (http://www.getcomposer.org) to manage dependencies, so the best way to get others to use your newly created bundle is to make it available through composer. To do so, we add a simple composer.json file to our bundle as follows:

```
{
    "name": "khepin/github-auth-bundle",
    "type": "symfony-bundle",
    "description": "Let your user authenticate to a Symfony2 app
      through their github account",
```

```
            "keywords": ["authentication, symfony, bundle, github"],
            "homepage": "http://xxxx.com",
            "license": "MIT",
            "authors": [
                {
                    "name": "Machete",
                    "homepage": "http://en.wikipedia.org/wiki/Machete_(film)"
                }
            ],
            "minimum-stability": "dev",
            "require": {
                "php": ">=5.3.2",
                "friendsofofsymfony/user-bundle": "~1.3"
            },
            {

                "mockery/mockery": "*"
            },
            {

                "autoload": {"psr-0": {"Khepin\\GithubAuthBundle": ""}}
            },
            {

                "target-dir": "Khepin/GithubAuthBundle"
            }
        }
    }
```

Once this is in place, you can register your package on `http://packagist.org`, and it will be available for download through composer.

Here, we included the MIT license. There are many existing open source licenses, and if you decide to open source your bundle, you should pick one (or know what it means when you don't). The `http://choosealicense.com/` website can help you decide which license is right for you. Symfony itself is MIT licensed, and this is a popular choice for many Symfony bundles.

Is it just a bundle?

A Symfony bundle is meant to be used only within Symfony. By making your code available as a bundle, you limit it to the people using the Symfony framework. The audience for whom you have created the bundle might actually be larger than that within the PHP world. In *Chapter 2, Commands and Templates*, we introduced the idea that commands in Symfony should only be a very thin wrapper around a service. Well, your bundle should also be a very thin wrapper when possible.

The example we followed in this chapter is for GitHub authentication. It is well suited as it is being fully packaged as a bundle due to the following reasons:

- It only deals with authentication in the Symfony way. Other frameworks or PHP without any framework will deal with authentication differently.

- There is very little logic that is not specific to Symfony. The only part where we do things not completely for Symfony is when we call the GitHub API, but it's contained within just 10 lines of code.

In many cases, your bundle will do more. Maybe, instead of just dealing with the authentication as we did here, you could add a full integration of GitHub. This would mean that based on a user, you can browse their repositories, notifications, latest comments, and so on. If you provide this through a bundle, you have most likely developed a complete API client. This will be very valuable for use outside of Symfony and should then be extracted to a separate library. Your bundle will then exist only to bridge the API client and the framework, provide authentication, declare the appropriate services, and so on.

There is no strict rule that suggests when something should or should not be in a bundle, but asking yourself the question whether some functionality could be extracted for reuse outside of Symfony will lead you on the right way!

Summary

With what we saw in all the previous chapters, you know how to craft Symfony extensions that will make your work easy to reuse within your project.

With this final chapter, you learned how to share it between projects, people, and teams. The technical part of creating a bundle that can be shared is relatively easy. Usually, your code will already be structured inside a bundle, and setting up the configuration and the extension is all you will have to worry about.

It is important to also take time to carefully prepare about the non-technical aspects of sharing a Symfony bundle such as documentation, licensing, and testing. This will greatly help your contributions to be noticed and spread among the community.

Index

Symbols

@Security annotation 77

A

B

C

user pictures
  resizing 28-31
user preferences
  updating, custom events used 20-23
User Provider block 64
UserProvider class 69, 70
user_provider parameter 66
user response
  generating, with listeners 24, 25

V

validator 81
version, Doctrine
  about 96-98
  setting 98, 99
  testing 101
  updating 100
  using 100
vote method 72
voter
  about 72
  ACCESS_ABSTAIN 74
  ACCESS_DENIED 74
  ACCESS_GRANTED 74
  VoterInterface method 72
VoterInterface methods
  supportsAttribute method 72
  supportsClass method 72
  vote method 72

Thank you for buying
Extending Symfony2 Web Application Framework

About Packt Publishing

Packt, pronounced 'packed', published its first book "*Mastering phpMyAdmin for Effective MySQL Management*" in April 2004 and subsequently continued to specialize in publishing highly focused books on specific technologies and solutions.

Our books and publications share the experiences of your fellow IT professionals in adapting and customizing today's systems, applications, and frameworks. Our solution based books give you the knowledge and power to customize the software and technologies you're using to get the job done. Packt books are more specific and less general than the IT books you have seen in the past. Our unique business model allows us to bring you more focused information, giving you more of what you need to know, and less of what you don't.

Packt is a modern, yet unique publishing company, which focuses on producing quality, cutting-edge books for communities of developers, administrators, and newbies alike. For more information, please visit our website: www.packtpub.com.

About Packt Open Source

In 2010, Packt launched two new brands, Packt Open Source and Packt Enterprise, in order to continue its focus on specialization. This book is part of the Packt Open Source brand, home to books published on software built around Open Source licenses, and offering information to anybody from advanced developers to budding web designers. The Open Source brand also runs Packt's Open Source Royalty Scheme, by which Packt gives a royalty to each Open Source project about whose software a book is sold.

Writing for Packt

We welcome all inquiries from people who are interested in authoring. Book proposals should be sent to author@packtpub.com. If your book idea is still at an early stage and you would like to discuss it first before writing a formal book proposal, contact us; one of our commissioning editors will get in touch with you.

We're not just looking for published authors; if you have strong technical skills but no writing experience, our experienced editors can help you develop a writing career, or simply get some additional reward for your expertise.

Laravel Application Development Blueprints

ISBN: 978-1-78328-211-1   Paperback: 260 pages

Learn to develop 10 fantastic applications with the new and improved Laravel 4

1. Learn how to integrate third-party scripts and libraries into your application.

2. With different techniques, learn how to adapt different methods to your needs.

3. Expand your knowledge of Laravel 4 so you can tailor the sample solutions to your requirements.

Mastering Web Application Development with AngularJS

ISBN: 978-1-78216-182-0   Paperback: 372 pages

Build single-page web applications using the power of AngularJS

1. Make the most out of AngularJS by understanding the AngularJS philosophy and applying it to real life development tasks.

2. Effectively structure, write, test, and finally deploy your application.

3. Add security and optimization features to your AngularJS applications.

Please check **www.PacktPub.com** for information on our titles

Persistence in PHP with Doctrine ORM

ISBN: 978-1-78216-410-4   Paperback: 114 pages

Build a model layer of your PHP applications successfully, using Doctrine ORM

1. Develop a fully functional Doctrine-backed web application.

2. Demonstrate aspects of Doctrine using code samples.

3. Generate a database schema from your PHP classes.

Learning FuelPHP for Effective PHP Development

ISBN: 978-1-78216-036-6   Paperback: 104 pages

Use the flexible FuelPHP framework to quickly and effectively create PHP applications

1. Scaffold with oil - the FuelPHP command-line tool.

2. Build an administration quickly and effectively.

3. Create your own project using FuelPHP.

Please check **www.PacktPub.com** for information on our titles

Made in the USA
Lexington, KY
27 April 2016